CATHEDRALS
AND ABBEY CHURCHES
OF THE RHINE

CATHEDRALS
AND
ABBEY CHURCHES
OF THE RHINE

ERNST GALL

TRANSLATED AND ADAPTED BY OLIVE COOK

PHOTOGRAPHS BY H. SCHMIDT-GLASSNER

200 monochrome plates
28 architectural drawings and plans

THAMES AND HUDSON · LONDON

FIRST PUBLISHED IN GREAT BRITAIN 1963
ALL RIGHTS RESERVED
THIS BOOK MUST NOT BE IMPORTED FOR SALE INTO THE U.S.A.
TEXT PRINTED IN THE NETHERLANDS BY JOH. ENSCHEDÉ EN ZONEN
ILLUSTRATIONS PRINTED IN GERMANY BY KASTNER & CALLWEY MUNICH

CONTENTS

INTRODUCTION

There are more cathedrals and abbey churches in the Rhineland than in any other part of Germany. All the more ancient of these foundations, including Strassburg, Speyer, Worms, Mainz and Cologne, are on the left bank of the river which was culturally more developed than the right, for it formed the boundary of the Roman Empire and Christianity was accepted earlier there than on the right bank. After the final overthrow of the West Roman Empire under the Merovingian Clovis (486) the Germanic peoples became the rulers of the Rhineland. The territories along the lower and middle reaches of the river were colonised by the Franks while the valleys of the Upper Rhine were occupied by the Swabians, a disposition which had important consequences architecturally for the two races differed sharply from one another in temperament and vision. Their descendants were, however, alike in their desire to preserve the monuments of the Middle Ages in the Rhineland, and never succumbed to that passion for rebuilding which during the Baroque period deprived most of the medieval churches of Bavaria and East Swabia of their medieval character. We are therefore largely dependent for our knowledge of Carolingian and German Romanesque and Gothic architecture upon the buildings on the Rhine. The ancient centre of artistic inspiration was in the west and the reforms carried out by the Cistercians and the Hirsau monks strengthened the importance of this cultural centre, which again became prominent during the Gothic period. The few ecclesiastical buildings in the Rhineland which date from the Baroque period, derive their inspiration on the other hand from the south.

EARLY CHRISTIAN PERIOD

The chief remains of Early Christian churches in the Rhineland are incorporated in the Cathedral at Trèves and in the Abbey Church of St Gereon at Cologne. Parts of the walls of these two great buildings date from Roman times.

Trèves was begun in the early part of the 4th century and the first impressive structure consisted of two adjacent churches the ground plans of which were re- *fig. 1* vealed by excavation during the years 1943–52. The city was founded by the Emperor Augustus, and under Diocletian it became the capital of the West Roman Empire, the seat of Maximinian, Constantius Chlorus and his consort Helena and, for a time, of their son Constantine. The Empress Helena was baptised a Christian in 313 and the Cathedral was built between 324 and 348. Of the two adjoining churches the northern building was triple-aisled with a square forecourt. According to the most recent finds the chancel was square-ended and of the same width as the main aisle. The choir lay immediately beyond the nave, marked off from the body of the church by two pillars, and on either side of it were two square chambers, probably sacristies. The other rather narrower church was also furnished with a forecourt, but between this and the actual entrance to the church was a rectangular basilican portico alongside which, connecting the two churches, was the baptistery. The eastern termination of this church too, was square and, like the chancel of its neighbour, it included square side chambers.

The reason for the existence of the two churches side by side is not known. The one to the south later became the parish church, thus exemplifying the distinction made throughout the Middle Ages between the clergy and the people and which explains the frequent occurence of a parish church and a baptistery in the immediate vicinity of a cathedral. It became customary to distinguish the chancel of an episcopal church, the space set aside for the clergy and choir, by the splendour of its architecture from the simple nave where the people worshipped; and it was for this

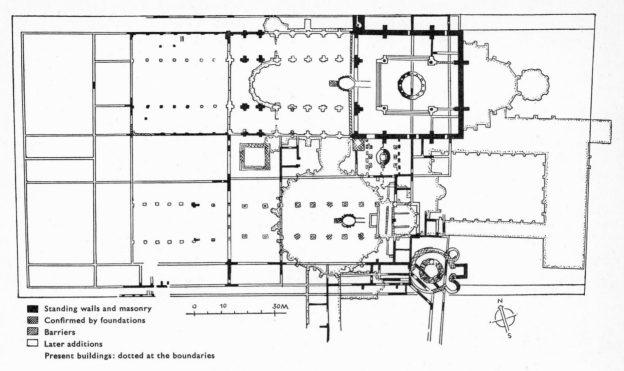

Fig. 1　Trèves, Cathedral. Ground-plan of the earliest layout based
on the excavations carried out by Theodor Konrad Kempf.

reason that the Emperor Gratian (375–383) carried out extensive alterations in the
northern church at Trèves. The relatively simple sanctuary was replaced by a most
impressive composition with four mighty columns supporting a central structure.
Beneath this was the stepped altar base and a polygonal pillared arrangement, the
purpose of which is not yet definitely known. However the part of the church
allocated to the clergy was now properly differentiated from the nave. The latter
was at this time provided with galleries which were probably intended for the
female members of the congregation.

The Cathedral was severely damaged during the succeeding period of change and
upheaval, but was rebuilt in the 6th century by Bishop Nicetius. There were no
important changes in the plan except that the forecourt of the northern church was
abandoned. After the destruction caused by the Norman invasion of 882 the only
part of the episcopal church that was restored was Gratian's sanctuary, while the

parish church, which was dedicated to the Virgin Mary, was rebuilt to incorporate the old chancel with a new simple nave. It remained unaltered until the 13th century. Parts of Gratian's sanctuary still survive in the fabric of the episcopal church in the form of arches of sandstone and courses of Roman brickwork.

Cologne, originally a smaller town than Trèves, had become Christian by the beginning of the 4th century. The 13th century oval nave of the Abbey Church of *pls. 190, 191* St Gereon was constructed on the ground plan of its predecessor, the foundation of *fig. 2* which is attributed to the Empress Helena. Excavations have shown that the Early Christian oval, the longer sides of which were each composed of four semicircular arched recesses, opened towards the east into a larger apsidal recess containing the altar and towards the west into a rectangular porch with side apses. The oval had a flat roof and round-headed windows.

Cologne Cathedral goes back to the time of Bishop Maternus, but the original foundation was destroyed in 355 when the Franks took Cologne. Bishop Severinus

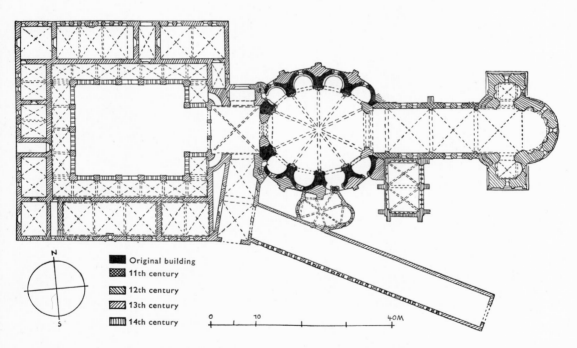

Fig. 2 Cologne, St Gereon. Ground-plan of the church with the
former monastery (after Boisserée).

then appears to have turned his residence in the Hohen Strasse into an episcopal church. It consisted of a porch, an aisleless nave and a western apse. This simple plan was retained until 870.

The Early Christian churches of the Rhineland belong to a period when architects were confronted by completely new problems. The Roman palaces and baths, remains of which are still to be seen at Trèves, could indeed accommodate vast assemblies, but the purpose of the church was not only to hold large numbers but to give aesthetic expression to the aspirations of the new faith, to proclaim the glory of the world to come rather than to celebrate the splendour of the world we know. The temple of pagan antiquity was conceived as a shrine from which the public was excluded, and relied for effect on the magnificence of its exterior; but in the Early Christian church the interior was of supreme importance and the exterior was simple and insignificant.

From the discoveries made at St Gereon's, Cologne, we know that Early Christian church interiors in this region were richly decorated with columns and mosaics and that the chancel was sufficiently emphasised to concentrate the attention of the faithful. Very soon this part of the church was to be accentuated not only inside the church but externally as well.

THE CAROLINGIAN PERIOD

The fact that so little Carolingian work has survived lends special interest to the well preserved chapel at Aix-la-Chapelle. It was built for Charlemagne as his royal *pls. 158–163* mausoleum towards the end of the 8th century and was consecrated in 805 by Pope Leo III. Recent discoveries have proved that the chapel was erected on the foundations of Roman baths containing an apsidal hall which could readily be converted into a church. Charlemagne's chapel is a polygon of sixteen sides every *fig. 3* two angles of which converge on to one pier thus forming a lofty central internal octagon surrounded by a two-storeyed aisle. The aisle vaults are groined, but the galleries above them are barrel vaulted. To the east of the octagon in place of the present chancel there was originally a two-storeyed square-ended sanctuary containing two altars. To the west is a two-storeyed vaulted porch flanked by staircase turrets. This was altered in the 14th century and again in the 19th century when the western steeple was added. The galleries above the central octagon were added after a fire in 1224 and the outer roof of the octagon dates from 1664.

The old Carolingian building is today surrounded by numerous chapels dating from the Gothic and Baroque periods, but in the 9th century there were only two chapels, both galleried and rectangular in shape, one on the north, the other on the south side. In front of the chapel to the west was a forecourt from the north eastern corner of which a long colonnade led to the hall of the Imperial Palace.

Some of the antique columns of the octagon were brought to Aix-la-Chapelle from Ravenna, a fact which strengthens the probability that the architect of the chapel was inspired by S. Vitale. Yet the two buildings differ in several respects. S. Vitale is octagonal both within and without, the sanctuary consists of only one storey and the building is roofed with a cross vault. The architect of Aix-la-Chapelle flattened the curved-out niches into which the central octagon of S. Vitale expands and eliminated the columns on the ground floor so that simple wide openings

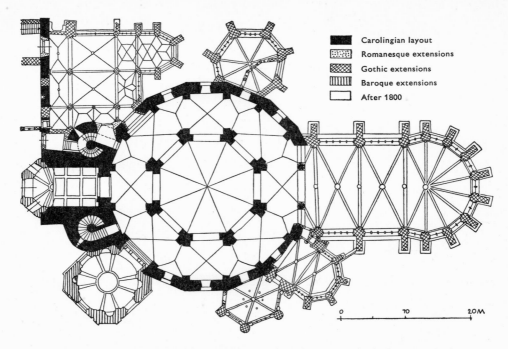

Fig. 3   Aix-la-Chapelle, former Palatine chapel, now cathedral, ground-plan.

alternate with short, sturdy piers. The plainness and massiveness of this ground floor
make an utterly different impression from the subtle spacial harmonies of S. Vitale,
though the upper floors with their polished columns superimposed in two orders
do recapture something of the strange sensation of weightlessness which characterises Justinian's church. Of the fittings and decorations of Charlemagne's time nothing remains except the fine bronze railings of the galleries. The octagon vault was
once embellished with a great mosaic and there were probably other mosaics in the
porch, sanctuary and window recesses. The present over ornate decoration dates
from the early 20th century.

Cologne Cathedral was consecrated in 870, but we can now only form the most
generalised picture of what it was like. Indeed, except for Aix-la-Chapelle, we have
no precise knowledge of the Carolingian cathedrals of the Rhineland. With regard
to monastic churches, however, the situation is more favourable. The church at
pl. 100 Lorsch was founded in 763, but the whole monastery was moved to higher ground

14

in 767 to escape the danger of floods; and, thanks to the generosity of Charlemagne a fine new church was consecrated in the presence of the Emperor in 774. Nothing alas, survives of this building, but excavations have made it possible to reconstruct its plan. The chancel was square-ended and the nave was aisled. The magnificent west end consisted of a triple-aisled entrance porch with a second choir on the first floor and a bell loft flanked by two staircase turrets. Beyond the west end stretched a wide forecourt with an ornate two-storeyed gatehouse which still stands and which, like the other surviving works of Charlemagne's Empire, marks the borderline between the Late Roman-Early Christian and the Romanesque styles. It is possible that this gatehouse was erected as a triumphal arch for Charlemagne after his victory over the Lombard King Desiderius.

The great church at Lorsch was altered several times in the course of the centuries. In about 880 a mausoleum in the form of an apsidal external crypt was added

fig. 4

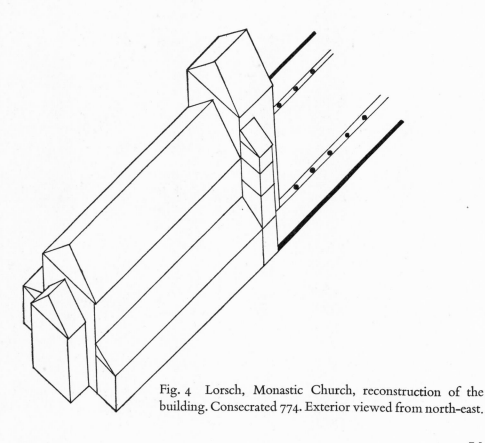

Fig. 4   Lorsch, Monastic Church, reconstruction of the building. Consecrated 774. Exterior viewed from north-east.

15

to the east end and Ludwig the German (d. 876) and his son Ludwig (d. 882) were buried there. The foundations of another chapel have been discovered to the south east. With its double choir, one in the normal position at the east end, the other at the west end, Lorsch provides an early example of a feature which is only found in churches north of the Alps and which is particularly common in the Rhineland.

The builders of other Carolingian churches were satisfied with a single choir. Among them the former Benedictine church of St Justinus at Höchst is of special interest because the whole of the lower part of the Carolingian nave has been preserved. The short, massive pillars with their splendid Corinthian capitals and richly grooved imposts derive from antique example but are treated in an original manner. The proportions are no longer classical, the carving is curiously abstract and the accent, as at Aix-la-Chapelle, is on mass.

Owing to the shortage of stone suitable for columns, piers were often used in Rhenish basilicas. The oldest surviving examples of this use are to be found at Steinbach and Seligenstadt, where the abbey churches both owe their existence to Einhart, Charlemagne's friend and biographer. At Steinbach, completed in 827, the main aisle, the apsidal chancel, the northern side chapel and the remarkable cruciform crypt all survive. Einhart and his wife Imma are said to have been buried in this crypt. Seligenstadt (831–840) has recently been restored as far as possible to its original condition. It consists of a broad aisled nave, transepts and an apse with an ambulatory, from which a vaulted passage leads down to the tomb, underneath the crossing, of the martyrs Marcellinus and Peter, whose relics had been secured by Einhart in Rome.

pls. 176, 177

fig. 5

The east end of the important abbey church of Werden was also built around a tomb, though here it was originally outside the church just beyond the chancel. It contained the remains of Bishop Ludger who had founded the church in 804. After his death the church was enlarged to incorporate the tomb and consecrated anew in 875. The present position of the tomb is in the crypt immediately beneath the high altar. The Carolingian crypt has been preserved although the rest of the church was rebuilt after a fire in 1256. An external chapel had been added to the actual crypt for the tombs of Ludger's relatives and successors and during the 11th century this chapel was rebuilt with three aisles of equal height and the walls were enriched with

16

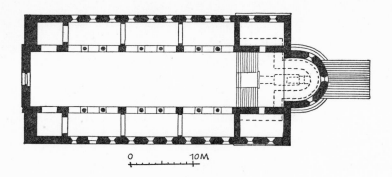

Fig. 5 Werden, reconstruction of the ground plan of the Abbey church consecrated 875 (after W. Effmann).

numbers of niches all containing windows. The ambulatory of the older crypt is also adorned with niches. Niches, as we have seen, played an important part in the Early Christian church of St Gereon at Cologne and they soon became a traditional feature of Lower Rhenish churches.

Ludger's church was triple-aisled but we have no precise knowledge of how it was terminated either to the east or the west. When the building was enlarged to embrace Ludger's tomb the choir was lengthened, raised up over the crypt and furnished with two-storeyed transepts. Close to the church on the south side was a chapel dedicated to St Stephen which some experts regard as Ludger's original church. It had a central tower and the east end and the transepts all terminated in apses of equal size, a common arrangement in churches of the Lower Rhineland.

The monastery at Werden served a large parish and a special church (completed in 943) was therefore built for christening and marriage services. It was surmounted by a central tower and a gallery ran round the barrel vaulted nave and transepts. The west end was drastically altered in succeeding periods but we know that it was flanked by staircase turrets giving access to the galleries and that there was an ante-chamber and a projecting porch.

The Carolingian church of St Castor at Coblenz, which was consecrated by <abbr>pls. 130, 131</abbr> Archbishop Hetti of Trèves in 836, was entirely rebuilt in the 13th century, but the lower storey of the original west end still stands, showing that the design consisted of a crossing without a tower and a galleried entrance porch of the same width as the nave. Carolingian west ends assume various forms but are always important. When they were only required to include a gallery for a choir or an oratory for church

17

dignitaries a comparatively modest plan sufficed, but when the west end was to contain a second sanctuary, as at Lorsch, a building of imposing proportions was called for.

The churches built on the island of Reichenau in Lake Constance occupy a special place in the history of Carolingian architecture. The Anglo-Saxon missionary Bishop Pirmin founded a monastery on the island in 724. Pirmin's small aisleless church was replaced under Abbot Hatto by a much larger cruciform building which was consecrated in 816. Part of the chancel survives showing it to have been almost square with two adjoining terminal apses such as occur nowhere else. The aisled nave was strikingly short and there was a low tower over the crossing. Abbot Hatto built a little cell for himself on the east side of the island where he lived in solitary contemplation until his death in 823; a church dedicated to St George was built over this cell by Abbot Hatto III between 890 and 896. The cell became the square crypt and above it was a square-ended sanctuary. The rest of the building took the form of a triple-aisled basilica with rectangular transepts and a tower over the crossing. The west end of the central aisle terminated in an apse

pls. 1–6
fig. 6
pls. 7–11

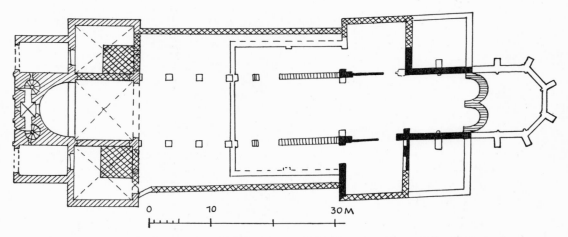

Black: Crossing (choir) and sanctuarium of building consecrated 816. The extent of the nave indicated by broken lines.
Horizontal: Excavated double apse of the building consecrated 816
Cross-hatched: Extensions carried out under Abbot Witigowo about 990
Diagonal: West choir of Abbot Berno 1030–48
Vertical: Reconstruction (Extension of the choir into the nave)

Fig. 6   Reichenau-Mittelzell, Monastery Church.

for a second altar. The crypt is the most interesting part of the church. Steps and a short passage lead down from the raised choir to a long central corridor opening into the crypt which is divided by four columns into three compartments of equal height. It is therefore one of the earliest of the typically German "hall" crypts.

Bishop Egino of Verona, who was a native of the Lower Rhineland, founded a cell on the west side of Reichenau above which a small church was built when he died in 802. It was probably a short, aisled structure with an eastern apse. All the churches built on Reichenau during the 8th and 9th centuries were very small, as the number of monks in so isolated a place was never high.

The remains of Carolingian churches are too incomplete to provide a clear picture of their character as works of art. The importance of the tower is however obvious, its purpose being to emphasise the part of the church set aside for the sanctuary and the clergy. Externally these Carolingian churches appear to have been extremely simple. Rich capitals crowning half-columns or shafts only occur in the west end of the Abbey Church of St Castor at Coblenz and in the gatehouse at Lorsch. The interior was lit from above and the rhythm of arch and support at once directed the attention of the entrant towards the sanctuary and altar. The absence of the horizontal architrave common in the older Italian basilicas above the columns dividing nave and aisles, and the introduction of arcade-arches intensified the rhythmic character of the interior. Carolingian churches were conspicuous for their great breadth; the walls were without articulation and were usually plastered and decorated with frescoes. Alternating dark and light stones sometimes added variety to arches, as at Aix-la-Chapelle. When the arcade-arches are supported by columns the capitals are generally elaborately carved as at Höchst. The device of the double choir heightened the solemn effect of the interior when at Mass the chanting of the monks echoed to and fro from both ends of the church.

After the decay of the Carolingian Empire during the 9th century the Rhineland was plundered by the Normans and attacked by the Magyars. The Cathedral of Trèves suffered heavily. The country, united under Charlemagne, split up into small principalities and even the monasteries were affected by the lack of a central authority and could do little to alleviate the state of continual strife which distracted the people. There was no cultural development until after Otto had been crowned

Holy Roman Emperor in 962 and had once more established a united Germany. His power is reflected not only in the extent of his empire but in the number of important buildings erected in his dominions. Ecclesiastical architecture in particular was given fresh impetus by the grant of more secular power to the church and gifts of land to its leaders.

Archbishop Bruno, brother of Otto I, founded a new Benedictine monastery, *pl. 189* St Pantaleon, at Cologne. It differed in only one respect from the buildings so far *fig. 7* considered. The nave, both internally and externally, was provided with a blind arcade, the round arches of which enclosed round-headed windows. This later became a feature of many Lower Rhenish churches.

The west end of Bruno's church was an elaborate structure with staircase turrets flanking a low central tower. Inside it took the form of transepts with a lofty central crossing opening through a great arch into the nave. The transepts and the western porch all had galleries supported by massive piers. There were small recesses for altars in the east walls of the transepts which indicates that the west end contained a second sanctuary. St Pantaleon was rebuilt during the 12th century as a triple-aisled church and the chancel was renovated in the late Gothic style in the 17th

Fig. 7   Cologne, St Pantaleon; reconstruction of the original exterior viewed from north-east.

20

century. The flat roofs of the west transepts were vaulted during the Romanesque period. The west porch was pulled down in the 18th century and the building was entirely restored in the 19th century.

The remaining portions of the 11th century church at Essen, which was turned into a "hall" church during the 13th century, are remarkable for the evidence they *pls. 174, 175* provide of an attempt to articulate and clarify space. The plan is highly original. The west end is dominated by a huge three-sided apse, a rectangle with bevelled corners, with a vault carried on lofty arches springing from massive piers. Broad round arches support the galleried upper floor, which consists of two superimposed orders, the two upper columns of which, most curiously to an English eye, meet the crown of the vaulting arch. The crossing is surmounted by an octagonal tower. The chancel comprises transepts and a sanctuary terminating in a five-sided apse above a "hall" crypt, and a two-storeyed external crypt onto which a rectangular mausoleum was built for the Abbess Theophanu. The crypt walls are enlivened by niches and the piers are most elaborately moulded. Originally there was a forecourt at the west end with a parish church on the west side of it. The conventual buildings lay to the north of the great church.

The western apse at Essen is reminiscent of Charlemagne's chapel at Aix-la-Chapelle. Another church, that of Ottmarsheim on the Upper Rhine, consecrated *pls. 26, 27* by Pope Leo IX in 1049, is not only inspired by the chapel, but so closely modelled on it that it differs from it only in a few details.

The churches of the Upper and Lower Rhine exhibit great divergences in conception and this is nowhere so clearly shown as in the alterations to the abbey of Mittelzell on the island of Reichenau which were carried out under Abbot *pls. 1–6* Witigowo (c. 990) and Abbot Berno (1030–48). Abbot Witigowo was responsible *fig. 6* for the present broad proportions of the nave and aisles and Abbot Berno enlarged the west end, adding transepts, a projecting porch and a monumental tower containing an apse for the altar. The interior of this whole western choir was austere and massive in character. The stone arches were slightly variegated in colour, but the walls were quite plain. Externally the centre of interest was the cube-like tower which apart from a single window and belfry lights, was articulated only by the simplest pilaster strips and blind arcading. Despite alterations such as the insertion

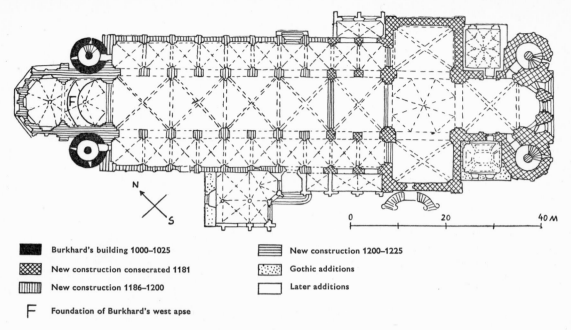

■ Burkhard's building 1000–1025   ▤ New construction 1200–1225

▨ New construction consecrated 1181   ⬚ Gothic additions

▥ New construction 1186–1200   ▢ Later additions

F   Foundation of Burkhard's west apse

Fig. 8   Worms Cathedral, ground-plan.

of circular window openings in 1688, the nave with its great piers is still essentially the work of Abbot Witigowo, spacious, yet heavily enclosed and controlled by the thick plain walls.

A column, which still stands in the opening between the west transepts and the south aisle, indicates that the nave at Mittelzell was originally furnished with *pls. 7–11* columns instead of piers. The Church of St George at Oberzell still retains all its original columns despite alterations carried out at the end of the 10th century. At that time apses were added to the east end and to the aisles and a two-storeyed narthex was built onto the apse at the west end. The splendidly preserved frescoes on the nave walls all date from this period.

pls. 12–16 The church at Niederzell, built over the cell of Bishop Egino, was enlarged during the 11th and 12th centuries so that the original building became the choir. The apses were changed into square-ended compartments and towers were erected over the side apses. The new nave was a simple basilica with piers separating the three aisles and a rectangular porch. But the whole aspect of the church was changed in the 18th century when the choir and nave were vaulted, new windows were inserted and the interior was completely redecorated in the Rococo style.

Of the cathedrals built in the time of Otto I little survives. The Carolingian foundation at Worms was replaced by a vast new church with a double choir and was consecrated by Bishop Burchard in 1081. The lower storeys of the round towers *fig. 8* which flanked Bishop Burchard's western apse and the base of the square-ended eastern sanctuary form part of the late Romanesque Cathedral we know today. One or two fragments of old masonry in the south transept of the east end indicate that Burchard's church had transepts.

While it is possible to attempt some reconstruction of the aspect of Worms at the beginning of the 11th century, the surviving fragments of that period at Mainz and the results of excavations can be interpreted in a bewildering variety of ways. It is not even certain exactly where the original Frankish cathedral was situated. The actual remains all come from Archbishop Willigis' church which was destroyed

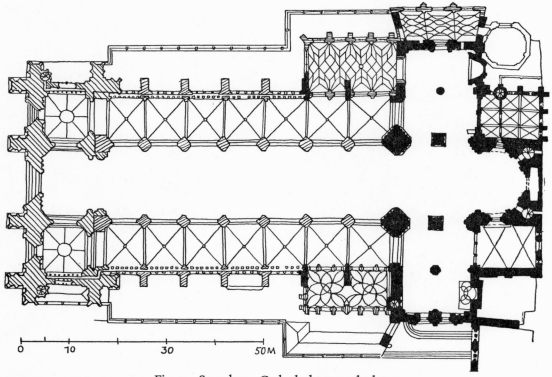

Fig. 9 Strassburg Cathedral, ground-plan.

by fire in 1009. They seem to indicate a triple-aisled basilica with long western transepts. The form of the western sanctuary is not precisely known. Traces of an apse have been found at the east end.

fig. 9 Strassburg Cathedral was begun in 1015 by Bishop Werinher of Habsburg. It was of impressive proportions as we know from the later Gothic cathedral erected on the old foundations. Intensive study of the foundations and those portions of the 11th century walls which still stand permit a fairly accurate reconstruction of the original ground plan. The triple-aisled basilica had an extensive east end with wide transepts. The choir was in the crossing and the sanctuary was apsidal. Externally the east end took the form of a mighty rectangular tower; beneath it was the "hall" crypt essentially as it is today. On either side of the sanctuary were two-storeyed chapels or sacristies connected to it by narrow spiral staircases. The external walls of these chapels formed a straight line with the east wall of the tower. The immense breadth of the nave was typically Upper Rhenish. The twin-towered west facade is one of the earliest examples of the elaborate west fronts which later became general. Its origin lies without doubt in the still earlier emphasis on the whole west end, which at Strassburg is less marked than in many Rhenish churches because there was apparently no need there for a double sanctuary as at Worms and Mainz. When there was a double choir, as at Essen, there was generally a high tower over the crossing with lower flanking towers. When there was no western choir the central tower was abandoned and the side towers were given a more monumental form.

pls. 24, 25 The Minster at Basle, which was consecrated in 1019, probably had a twin-towered facade like that of Strassburg. The two lower storeys of the northern tower still stand.

pls. 18–23 The Minster at Constance, an early foundation, reveals traces in the "hall" crypt of the building which was redesigned by Bishop Lambert (995–1018). The heavy cushion capitals of the short columns are decorated all over with lightly carved acanthus leaves. A few fragments of early 11th century masonry suggest that Bishop Lambert's church had a square crossing, which served as the choir, and small rectangular transepts. The nave was probably a flat-roofed basilica with columns.

THE ROMANESQUE PERIOD

The remains of Rhenish churches of the late Ottonian period are scanty and are far surpassed by the surviving works built under the Salian Emperors (1024–1137). Conrad II founded the Benedictine monastery of Limburg in 1025 and appointed as Abbot Poppo of Stablo, an advocate of monastic reform. Today only a ruin testifies to the former size and splendour of the church. Parts of the crypt, chancel, transepts and the west end of the 11th century structure have been preserved and the external walls of the nave are also still standing. The crossing, which was surmounted by a short octagonal tower, was square and in each of the transepts there was an apsidal altar recess in the east wall. The chancel was square-ended and there was a crypt underneath it. The west end consisted of a vaulted porch with a gallery above it which may have been used either by the choir or the royal family. This porch lay immediately in front of the central aisle; the side aisles terminated towards the west in square, two-storeyed chambers which were probably surmounted by towers, though some experts believe that the central porch was higher than the flanking structures. Beyond the west end was a rectangular forecourt. The aesthetic character of the tall, narrow building was determined by the great height of the nave and transepts with their double array of windows.

At Speyer the very position of the Cathedral proclaims its importance. The west front rises up at the end of the main street, dominating the town, while the east end *pls. 67–75* soars above the Rhine and must in medieval times have attracted the reverent gaze of all who passed along the busy waterway. The Cathedral was founded on the site of an older building by Conrad II who intended it as a burial place for himself and his descendants, and rulers were actually interred here until the 14th century. When the town was sacked in 1689 the fame of the Cathedral was so great that it was spared by the special command of Louis XIV. It nevertheless caught fire and was destroyed except for the wall of the south aisle, the east end of the

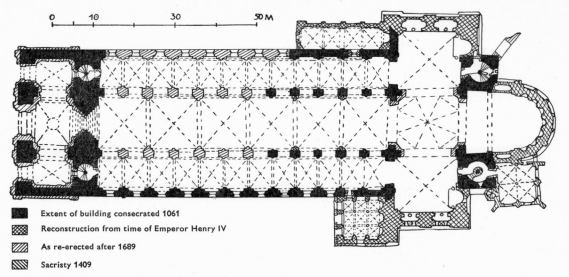

Extent of building consecrated 1061
Reconstruction from time of Emperor Henry IV
As re-erected after 1689
Sacristy 1409

Fig. 10   Speyer Cathedral, ground-plan.

fig. 10 nave and part of its vault and the ground floor of the west end. It was restored in its original form by Ignaz Michael Neumann in 1772–78. To anyone conversant with English architecture this must appear an extraordinary fact. It would not have occurred to any English architect of that time to restore a medieval building, especially a Romanesque building, in its original style. One has only to think of Wyatt's work at Salisbury. Speyer was again in danger during the Napoleonic wars and would certainly have been demolished if Napoleon himself had not intervened. The west end was unsuccessfuly restored in the 19th century.

fig. 11   The most interesting part of the 11th century building was the immensely long, narrow nave. It made an impression of verticality which was emphasised by the treatment of the walls. The divisions of the twelve bays were marked by piers rising to the height of some 40 feet. Eight shafts were attached to each pier and from the abaci supporting the narrow arcade-arches sprang engaged columns, so that the walls were powerfully articulated. The engaged columns soared up to form recessed arches enclosing the clerestory windows.

The plan of the long chancel can be deduced from that of the surviving "hall" crypt which was immediately beneath it. It was about 10 feet higher than the nave

26

and included transepts, a crossing which served as the choir and was marked by a tower, and an apsidal sanctuary. There were additional towers in the corners between the transepts and the sanctuary. The crypt consisted of three chambers of equal height separated by piers, and an apsidal east end containing an altar. The side chambers were each furnished with three small apsidal altar recesses to the east, so that altogether there were no less than seven altars in the crypt. To the west there was a narrow antechamber from which two steps led up through arched openings to the royal vault which was placed directly in front of the crossing. It is only possible to give a generalised picture of the west end. It was of the same width as the nave and boasted a splendid porch. The great recessed western portal was flanked by towers and above it rose an octagonal tower and belfry.

This impressive group was completed during the reign of Henry IV but soon

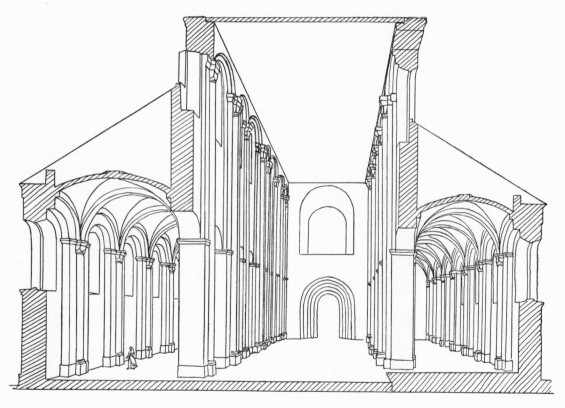

Fig. 11   Speyer Cathedral, reconstruction of the original layout
of the 11th century, looking towards the west.

after 1080 the Cathedral was in danger of collapse through floods and Henry sent for advice to Bishop Benno of Osnabrück, an experienced architect. The Bishop was in favour of extensive rebuilding and the work was eventually completed under Henry V. Fires in 1137 and 1159 resulted in further rebuilding.

Henry IV was not only concerned with the safety of the building: he desired that Speyer should surpass all other German cathedrals. The first task of the builders was to strengthen the foundations of the chancel and then to raise a completely new structure over them. The new apse was set on a powerful base pierced by the small round-headed windows of the crypt. Above the bold string-course dividing the base from the lofty upper stage rose tall half columns supporting blind arches within three of which were set round-headed windows. Directly below the roof line, not only of the apse but of the whole Cathedral, ran an eaves-gallery, a feature which probably originated in Northern Italy. The magnificent Corinthian capitals of this apse exterior and the exquisite mouldings of some of the windows were also distinctly Italian in feeling and it is possible that Henry IV employed a number of Italian workmen. The rich decoration of the new Cathedral contrasted sharply with the severity of the old building and inaugurated an innovation in style which soon spread to all the larger churches of the Rhineland. But the most important fact about the Cathedral architecturally was that not only the chancel but the entire nave was roofed with cross vaults. The height of the nave was increased and between each of the longitudinal arches a tiny round-headed window opened into the eaves-gallery. After the fire of 1159 a new octagonal tower was erected over the crossing and the transepts were ceiled with ribbed cross vaults.

pls. 114–123 Trèves Cathedral, which was begun by Archbishop Poppo and should have been completed under Archbishop Udo (1067-78), was not actually finished until 1121.
fig. 12 After the Norman invasion of 882 the east end could no longer be used for services. Archbishop Poppo (1016–47) replaced the four inner columns, two of which had been shattered, by much stouter cruciform piers and lengthened the building towards the west. A two-storeyed apse with an eaves-gallery and another arcaded gallery just below it occupied the centre of the west facade and arcade-galleries ran along the walls between the apse and the square flanking towers. The interior of Poppo's nave was redecorated in the Baroque style in the 18th century.

28

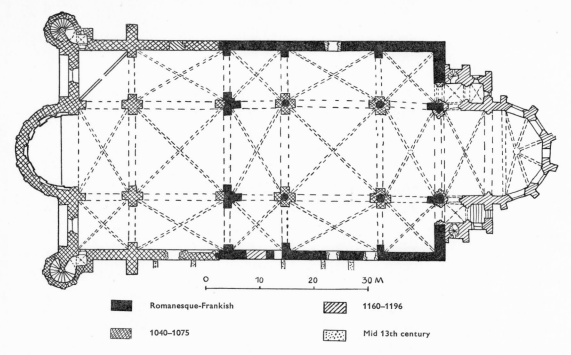

Fig. 12   Trèves Cathedral, ground-plan.

The Emperor Henry IV, who was so largely responsible for the rebuilding of *pls. 90–99* Speyer, also played a part in the restoration of Mainz Cathedral which had been severely damaged in a great fire in 1081. But when the Emperor died in 1106 parts of the Cathedral still stood in ruins. The nave and chancel had suffered most heavily, while the western choir, which was not renovated until the 13th century, was still in use. Owing to obvious resemblances between the eastern apse of Mainz and that of Speyer most experts are of the opinion that the east end was rebuilt earlier than the nave. The chancel apse of Mainz is not only very similar in structure to that of Speyer but the decorative features have so much in common that it seems more than likely that craftsmen from Lombardy worked on both buildings.

It is not easy to decide exactly what form the nave took at the end of the 11th century. The present groined vaults of the north and south aisles and ribbed cross vaults of the main aisle are of later date. We only know that Archbishop Adalbert I gave the new building a magnificent roof ("magnificum tectum"). Building operations are mentioned for the years 1183–96 and 1233, and in 1239 a consecration ceremony took place in the presence of the Emperor Conrad IV. But the new western choir could not have been completed by that date for it was not consecrated until 1243. The massive nave piers, which date from soon after the fire of 1081, support small, simple arches and a wall articulated by blind arcading. A half column rising to the crown of the blind arcading is attached to every second pier. The cushion capitals of these half columns serve as supports for the cross ribs and the transverse and longitudinal arches. Simple half columns are not used in any other part of the church to carry a ribbed cross vault. The present vault with its pointed transverse arches dates from the beginning of the 13th century, so the character of the original design is not at once apparent. For a simple cross vault not only half columns but also engaged piers were generally used. Both the form of the half columns and the great strength of the piers and the walls point to a barrel vault. But this would have made the insertion of the windows above the arcading a very difficult process. So probably the nave was flat-roofed to begin with and cross vaults were only introduced after the upper part of the walls had been rebuilt. The aisles were reconstructed at the end of the 12th century. The chancel, raised several steps above the nave, terminates in an apse containing the altar of St Stephen. The present neo-Romanesque tower over the crossing replaced a Gothic structure in 1869–79. The three-storeyed transepts have richly moulded portals and string-courses; the first floors contain sacristies and open through double arches to the choir, while the top storey is occupied by great galleries, the purpose of which is not known. The present crypt only dates from 1872-76.

The Romanesque work at Speyer and Mainz shows the style at its best. The stress on verticality and the use of pilasters and blind arcading to articulate the external walls distinguishes these buildings from the austere, broad, plain-walled designs of the 10th century. The interior also is dominated by a conception of form which is quite different from that of the antique tradition: the whole building is organised as a system of cubic units combining the use of towers with a basilican structure in a way which is foreign to Italian usage. The system of grouping together square compartments was most strikingly imposed on the interior when it became possible to roof the entire structure with stone vaults, to link the separate units into which walls and the space enclosed by them were divided and to impart a sweeping sense of rhythm to the whole. Decoration had formerly been limited to frescoes, but now a profusion of carved ornament graced capitals, mouldings and string-courses.

The churches of St Maria im Kapitol and St George at Cologne and the abbey church of All Saints at Schaffhausen were in course of construction at about the same time as the Salian Cathedral of Speyer. The convent church of St Maria im pls. 184, 185 Kapitol, which was destroyed during the last war, was probably founded at the end of the 7th century on the site of a late Roman secular building; but it was essentially a mid-11th century church and was consecrated in 1065. Part of the west end was of earlier date, perhaps 10th century. This west end consisted of a square central structure with galleries and a tower, flanked by octagonal staircase turrets. The two-storeyed, arcaded aisles were modelled on the aisle at Aix-la-Chapelle. The 11th century building comprised a triple-aisled basilican nave; the east end was erected on a trefoil plan with an ambulatory. The inspiration for this sanctuary was doubtless late Roman, where it had been used for mausolea and martyria.

Beneath the apses was a crypt with transepts and three chapels. As the church was built on a slope the east end, raised up over the crypt, was level with the nave. The ritual use of the three apses and the ambulatory is not known.

The chapels in the close vicinity of the church were probably intended for the use of the canonesses. A porch in front of the northern apse was connected with a chapel of St Nicholas adjoining the hospital and was obviously therefore used by the canonesses, while a porch leading into the southern apse provided an entrance for the canons who were appointed to every convent. This porch may also have been used for secular transactions. The cloisters leading to the living quarters of the canonesses and their pupils were immediately in front of the west end. The ambulatories and side aisles with their numerous altars were devoted to the processions which took place on every feast day in the Middle Ages.

The convent church of St George, which was founded by Archbishop Anno in 1059 and completed after 1067, was considerably simpler. The east end consisted of a chancel and transepts with a square crossing. The barrel-vaulted transepts were of singular design for they terminated externally in semi-hexagons, while inside they were semicircular with three lofty recesses. The sanctuary terminated in an apse which was divided on either side by three arches from long, narrow apsidal chapels and the apse was enriched by five niches and by windows set in arcading. The side chapels were raised up on account of the extensive, triple-aisled crypt underneath. The nave was aisled and there was a second apsidal choir at the west end, which was probably also enlivened by niches.

The Rhenish character of this church is apparent in the abundant use of niches, which gave additional variety to the trefoil plan. Here also the will to articulate and clarify space is dominant. St George's underwent extensive alterations in about 1140, when all the compartments were roofed with cross vaults. In order to achieve this the openings between the sanctuary and its side chapels were walled up and piers were introduced between the old columns of the nave. Towards the end of the 12th century the western apse was replaced by a square tower.

The little it has been possible to discover about the original church of the monastery at Schaffhausen, which was consecrated in 1064, is sufficient to show that it was utterly different in conception from the Frankish buildings on the Lower Rhine. The massive units of the composition were much more closely grouped. The short, aisled nave was no more than a connecting link between the east end and the western choir, both of which were imposing structures with transepts and twin towers. There was a forecourt at the west end and recent excavations have revealed the existence of a huge rhomboid shaped, walled courtyard behind the chancel, containing three chapels.

fig. 13   In 1087 after the monastery had been reorganised according to the stern asceticism of the Hirsau monks a new church was begun. It was completed in 1103 or 1104 and its extreme simplicity corresponded to the ideals of the Order. It was a square-ended basilica with plain walls and no sculpture, and there was no crypt, for the whole idea of devotions performed about altars and tombs hidden in mysterious subterranean gloom was abhorrent to the Hirsau monks. The church was therefore informed by an utterly different spirit from that which animated Speyer. It is a significant fact that no Hirsau monasteries were founded along the Lower Rhine. During the second half of the 12th century the chancel of All Saints was extended towards the east and in about 1200 a tower was built over the north transept of the west end, which was two-storeyed after the fashion of Cluniac churches and flanked by towers.

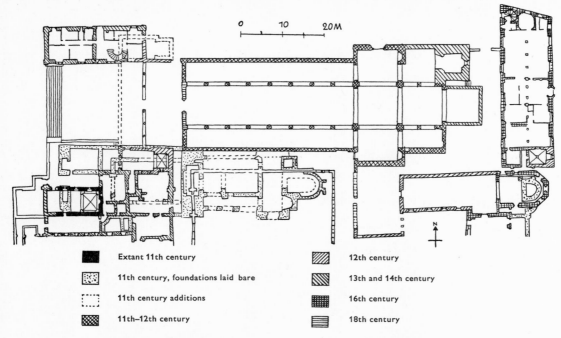

Fig. 13 Schaffhausen, Monastery, ground-plan of building
in its present state with excavated portions.

The remarkable church of Maria Laach on the Lower Rhine was almost exactly *pls. 140-143*
contemporary with All Saints, Schaffhausen. Seen from the wooded shores of the
lake above which it rises, the silhouette of the great six-towered church is awe-
inspiring, but it is even more impressive at close quarters. Its architectural members
of dark basalt stand out against the light walls.

Work on the church did not come to an end until the beginning of the 13th
century, but it was complete in all its essential features soon after 1093 when the
foundation stone was laid by the Count Palatinate Heinrich II and his consort
Adelheid. A short, aisled nave of five bays links an elaborate east end and a western
choir. The long eastern transepts contain apsidal niches in the east walls and between
these and the chancel apse slender turrets flank the octagonal tower over the crossing. The western transepts are narrow and do not project beyond the nave. Access
to the west gallery is from two sturdy round staircase turrets, and a bulky tower
surmounts the crossing. The western apse, which was used as a mausoleum, is two-
storeyed and there is a small forecourt beyond it.

33

The plan of 1093 did not provide for stone vaulting and it was only in the mid-12th century that it was decided to vault the nave. The present piers with their powerful attached shafts of black basalt were introduced at that time, but it was found that it was not possible to adopt the usual system of vaulting square compartments, and the architects were confronted with the problem of how to make the longitudinal and transverse arches the same height as the groins. As the pointed arch was not known in the Rhineland at the time, they surmounted the difficulty by stilting the longitudinal arches and flattening the transverse arches, a not altogether aesthetically satisfying solution. The nave, transepts and the central tower were all made higher during the 12th century. The nave was consecrated by Archbishop Hillin of Trèves in 1156, but the sanctuary was not completed until 1177.

Another but more modest church inspired by a similar attitude to ecclesiastical architecture is that of the Premonstratensian monastery of Knechtsteden which was *pls. 170–173* begun in 1138 and finished a few decades later, though the apse was rebuilt in the late 15th century. Except that there is no crypt the plan closely resembles that of Maria Laach. The basilican nave was intended from the first to carry vaults; it has four square compartments each consisting of two bays roofed with groined cross vaults and to the west it terminates in an apse. The piers are structurally different from those at Maria Laach; they have a square core buttressed by half columns on the side facing the nave and by three-quarter columns on all the other sides. The subsidiary cylindrical piers are perfectly plain with cushion capitals. The transverse arches of the side aisles spring rather oddly from narrow imposts above the abaci of the subsidiary piers. It is also curious that where the arcade-arches spring from the piers they are broader than the abaci. This all goes to show that the architect was not absolutely clear in his mind about the necessary strength of the supports.

A well moulded string-course runs above the arcade-arches, interrupted, however, by the vaulting shafts, and the clerestory windows are arranged in pairs. The walls were ornamented with frescoes, as at Maria Laach, and here and there with sculpture, of which a good example may be seen in the western apse. A magnificent recessed pilastered south porch giving access to the cloisters was added towards the close of the 12th century. Despite the exquisite detail of this porch, however,

34

the characteristic Lower Rhenish delight in ornament is not much in evidence at Knechtsteden, perhaps because of the severity of the Premonstratensian Order.

This delight emerges with full force in the Benedictine church at Brauweiler, which occupies a commanding position high above the surrounding landscape. *pls. 164, 165* Here the nave, though short, is of particular interest, for above the arcade-arches is a kind of rudimentary triforium, consisting of closely ranged niches and blind arches. There are three towers at either end of the church all overshadowed by the massive five-storeyed tower rising from the centre of the west front.

In 1135 a monastery at Eberbach was acquired by the Cistercians and they at once *pls. 109–113* set about rebuilding it in accordance with the austere ideals of their Order. The church, like all Cistercian foundations and unlike Benedictine monasteries, lay in a valley and was begun as a cruciform design with a square-ended chancel and three chapels on either side of the sanctuary. The work was interrupted and the church was not completed until 1186. The old ground plan was retained and so was the old metrical system of articulation. Despite alterations to some of the windows during the Gothic and Baroque periods the original character of the building has been well preserved. In the interior one is particularly conscious of the importance of the solid walls, both structurally and as a means of articulating space. The simple rectangular piers support plain round arches and are set so close together that there is no feeling of openness between the nave and aisles. The walls are without articulation except for the vaulting shafts and are pierced only by tiny round-headed windows just below the longitudinal arches of the vault. In the aisles the vaulting shafts rise directly from the ground instead of from the piers and thus impose a more emphatic rhythm on the structure, leading the eye on, which in the nave is encouraged to linger. The sense of enclosing walls is still stronger in the transepts, for the little chapels in the east walls are very low and the severely plain masonry above them is relieved by only one small window. The Cistercians did not favour the double choir and the church is square-ended to the west with a circular opening above two round-headed windows. Like all Cistercian foundations the church at Eberbach was originally intended exclusively for monks and novices. It was only later that the people were admitted and then a simple porch was added for their use on the south side. During the 14th century a series of chapels was built along the south aisle and in the Baroque period a square tower was built over the crossing with an onion dome and a lantern. The old Romanesque church had only a very modest little turret above the crossing.

Beside the buildings which have been described many monastic churches were erected at this time which had flat-roofed naves and vaulted aisles. A remarkable building of this type was the convent church of St Ursula in Cologne which was badly damaged in the last war. The nave, which is the first in the Lower Rhineland to have galleries, was probably built during the second quarter of the 12th century. It is not very long, but is articulated in a characteristically elegant, light, decorative manner. Above the round arcading run low galleries which were originally flat-roofed. Between the arcades are shallow pilaster strips which, before the Gothic vault was installed, reached to the top of the clerestory windows to form an ornamental band of blind arcading. Still more variety and detail were once imparted to the composition by colour.

The former abbey church of Murbach makes an indelible impression of grandeur though only the transepts and chancel are preserved. Two high square towers rise above the low transepts, but there is no tower over the crossing. To both the north and south these towers are accompanied by narrow two-storeyed wings, while to the east they open into the double-bayed side chapels of the sanctuary. The exterior *fig. 14* is richly decorated with blind arcadings and pilaster strips. The east end of the sanctuary is exceptionally well articulated by three broad horizontal divisions which become narrower towards the top. The second of these divisions displays pillars with ornate capitals springing from corbel heads. On either side of the central opening in the gable are carved reliefs while the cornice is handsomely corbelled. The gable of the south transept is treated in a similar way, several of the decorative motifs showing North Italian influence. Internally the entire structure is vaulted. The date of Murbach is not definitely established but it was probably begun in about 1135.

The concentration on the articulation of the walls which characterises this church is also the most striking feature of the Benedictine church of Marmontier. And another abbey church at Lautenbach exhibits the same tendency, though here the ornament is far simpler.

36

Fig. 14 Choir and sanctuary of the Abbey church in Murbach.

In about the middle of the 12th century there was tremendous building activity throughout the Rhineland. Many older churches were enlarged or entirely rebuilt. The congregrations had greatly increased and many of the churches were now pls. 190, 191 thrown open to the people. Thus the chancel and the old crypt of St Gereon's, fig. 2 Cologne, were lengthened so that the choir now included the former sanctuary. The new sanctuary consisted of a square bay with a cross vault to which Gothic ribs were added in the 14th century. It terminated in an apse and was flanked by rectangular towers which contained chapels articulated by niches in the lower storeys. The apse had two storeys enriched with closely set niches, blind arcading and three round-headed windows.

The external aspect of the tower-flanked apse is eloquent of the aesthetic characteristics of the Lower Rhine. While at Speyer on the Upper Rhine a monumental, single-storeyed apse rose from a low base, the apse of St Gereon is divided into three stages and is detailed and ornamental rather than monumental. The eaves-gallery, for instance, is much more elaborate than the one at Speyer.

Eaves-galleries made their first appearance in the Lower Rhineland in the small, pls. 152–157 exquisitely decorated double chapel consecrated in 1151 which the later Archbishop of Cologne, Arnold von Wied built on his own estate at Schwarzrheindorf. The exterior of this chapel, sparkling with the light and shade created by galleries, niches and infinitely varied mouldings, is among the most charming examples of the Lower Rhenish love of ornament.

While Cologne Cathedral had preserved its late Carolingian form with little change, extensive rebuilding was undertaken at Worms soon after the middle of the pls. 76–89 12th century. The early 11th century ground plan was retained in essentials, but the fig. 8 church was now to be vaulted throughout and made considerably higher. Octagonal towers crown the sancturies at either end and both east and west aspes are flanked by twin circular towers. The chancel was consecrated in 1181, while the nave and the western choir were completed only by the beginning of the 13th century. The interior of the sanctuary is apsidal but externally it ends in a straight wall running between the two flanking towers. The crossing serves as the choir and its powerful piers support pointed arches of three orders. The octagon of the tower rises on pendentives and is capped by an octagonal pointed roof each side of which is provided with a minute dormer. The sanctuary and transepts are roofed with ribbed cross vaults with partly round, partly stilted transverse arches. Many of the forms show a certain dependence on motifs found in Alsace and the Upper Rhineland. The connection is no less marked in the details of the exterior. Exactly the same roll moulding occurs, for instance, round the windows of the church at Lautenbach. The east end is characteristically decorated with an eaves-gallery, the columns of which rest on curiously carved corbels. Upon the window ledges crouch a variety of fantastic beasts and similar monsters peer from the plinths of piers and shafts in the interior.

The nave exhibits certain irregularities in the construction of the piers and the walls are slightly differently constituted. On the north side the blind arcading springs from the piers, while on the south side it only begins above the string-course dividing it from the arcade-arches. The north side is clearly earlier in date and the work of a different master. The vaults consist of simple transverse and longitudinal arches while the ribs are richly moulded after the French fashion. The aisles are roofed with plain cross vaults. The whole structure is still purely Romanesque with emphasis on the walls. Yet the west end shows some stylistic advance in the rich decoration that tends to break up the solidity of the walls. This is above all apparent in the walls of the picturesque polygonal apse which obviously belongs to the later stages in the evolution of the Romanesque style.

The rebuilding of the Minster at Basle which had been destroyed by fire in 1185, *pls. 24, 25* was well under way by 1205. The essential features of the late Romanesque building *fig. 15* have been preserved although an earthquake of 1356 brought down the upper part of the east end, the vault over the central aisle and the west towers. The flanking towers were not rebuilt but the rest of the damage was repaired in the Gothic period. Basle is the oldest building in the Rhineland to have an ambulatory round the sanctuary and it is also the oldest Rhenish church to be entirely roofed with a ribbed cross vault.

The ambulatory takes an unusual form: there is no floor on the sanctuary level, but the ambulatory runs right down to the crypt and is approached from the side aisles of the nave. Both the ambulatory and the nave are provided with galleries connected by a narrow passage in the transept walls. They can only be approached

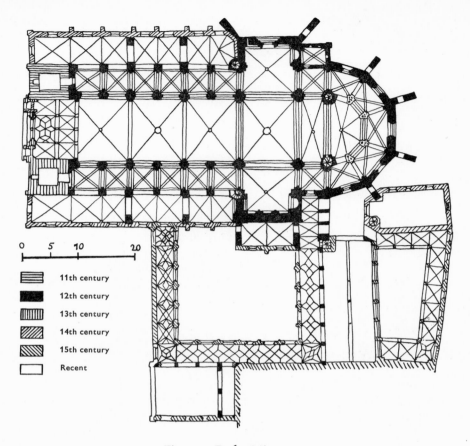

Fig. 15   Basle, Minster.

11th century
12th century
13th century
14th century
15th century
Recent

from the east side of the rood screen and were probably not accessible to the people in the Middle Ages. They were doubtless used by the choirs.

Architecturally Basle is no longer entirely Romanesque in feeling, for, in the interior, space is not only articulated by solid walls. The piers and subsidiary supports are designed to create a sense of movement and faintly foreshadow the Gothic system. This is borne out by the forward-swinging motion of the containing arches of the gallery-arcade and by the piers of the crossing which look almost like Gothic clustered columns. Basle is the work of an architectural school which though still rooted in the tradition of massive wall design, was influenced by French example in its attempts at new methods of articulating space as well as in its choice of some of the decorative motifs.

40

The Basle Minster had become an influential force in the Rhineland when, towards the end of the 12th century Bishop Werinher's 11th century cathedral at Strassburg was replaced by a new building. Already early in the 12th century the "hall" crypt below the sanctuary had been extended, an alteration which necessitated the raising of the crossing above the level of the nave and transepts. Plans for a new chancel were only made after this work had been begun so there was inevitably a certain loss of unity. An octagonal tower was raised over the crossing, but except for the lower part, this is now a work of 19th century restoration. The east wall of the transepts was rebuilt soon after the middle of the 12th century as was the double-arched entrance to the chapel of St Andrew in the south transept and the recess in the north transept containing the altar of St Lawrence. When the sanctuary was rebuilt the mighty lower walls of the tower which once crowned it were retained although internally the lower part of the apse was furnished with pointed niches and a small gallery. Massive vaulting piers and powerful corner columns were introduced to the east of the crossing and there were similar piers to the west. The transepts were shortened and given vaults so high that they were almost domical. The south transept was distinguished by features which showed an architectural advance on any church so far built in the Rhineland: it was lit by large traceried windows. Furthermore all the transept vaulting arches were of the same height and the central prop consisted of an octagonal column with attached shafts, no longer regarded as mere supports but soaring upwards to branch out in the ribs of the vault. Between the shafts stood slender figures of the Evangelists, trumpeting angels, angels bearing the instruments of the Passion and above them all Christ as Judge with the dead rising from their coffins at his feet. The sculptor of this column was already Gothic; he may have been a pupil in the workshop which was responsible for the transept portals of Chartres.

Several masters from different schools worked on the figures which adorned the portal of the south transept. Unfortunately they have only been partly preserved. The two spandrels containing reliefs of the Death and Coronation of the Virgin are old while the figures on the jambs of Ecclesia and the Synagogue, by the same master as the sculptures on the column, are copies of the originals which are now in the Strassburg Museum. The draped figures of the Apostles and the figure of

fig. 9

Solomon as Judge on the central column with the vision of Christ above his head are also new. The representation of Solomon suggests that medieval courts of justice were set up before the portal and this is corroborated by the records. The interior of the south transept was used for ecclesiastical transactions and for funeral services while the north transept was used for christenings.

The general character of the east end of Strassburg is still Romanesque, but the detail shows a new spirit, while in the later portions of the building Gothic structural elements have already made an appearance. Externally the most striking features are the massive corner buttresses.

pls. 28, 29 Among the late Romanesque churches of the Upper Rhine that of the former Benedictine monastery of St Fides at Schlettstadt is interesting on account of its design. The aisled nave consists of three square double bays with ribbed cross vaults over the nave while the aisles are roofed with simple groined vaults. The piers are provided with half-columns to carry the pointed arcade-arches and the transverse arches of the aisles. The transverse arches are rectangular in section and furnished with a simple moulding, while the ribs are flat with a roll moulding and rise from between the transverse and longitudinal arches, a device which occurs in Lorraine at Droiteval, Igney and Relanges, as does the ornamental form of the blind arcading. The architectural forms of the Romanesque period in the Upper Rhine and Lorraine are indeed basically identical. There is the same effect of breadth, the same variety of articulation in the treatment of walls and piers and the same general impression of heaviness. Decorative details are strongly sculptural and the ornamental motifs are often inspired by North Italian example.

pl. 188 The late Romanesque buildings of the Lower Rhine are entirely different in character. Among them the Church of the Apostles at Cologne is of particular fig. 16 importance. The original church dating from the early 11th century was a triple-aisled, flat-roofed basilica with western transepts and a square-ended western sanctuary surmounted by a square tower. The plan of the old east end is not known. It now consists of a square crossing crowned by an octagonal tower and lantern from which narrow barrel-vaulted bays open to north east and south all terminating in apses. In the corners between the apses are slender towers. The altar originally stood on the west side of the crossing immediately in front of the nave. This east end, though broad, creates a strong sense of enclosed space and radiates vitality. The two-storeyed apses are articulated by blind arcades, shallow niches, galleries and windows. There is the same liveliness in the treatment of the walls of the narrow bays in front of the apses. The articulation of walls by means of niches which is so marked a feature of this church might appear to be a development of the Lower Rhenish tradition of wall decoration, but here the motif is definitely used structurally. The niches and galleries of the Church of the Apostles are the expression of a conception of the church interior not as a series of units enclosed by walls but as a pattern of arches and supports. Such a conception was characteristic of northern

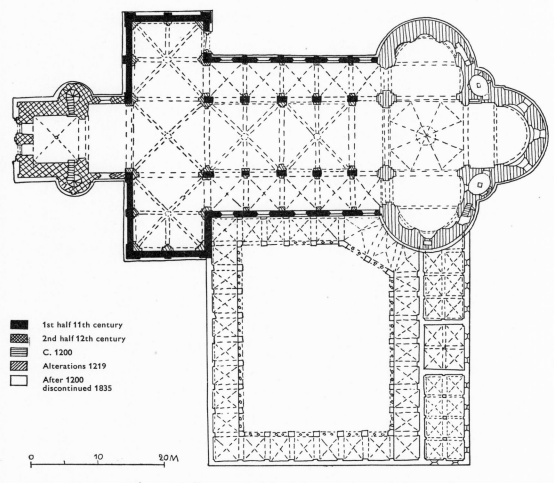

1st half 11th century
2nd half 12th century
C. 1200
Alterations 1219
After 1200
discontinued 1835

0   10   20M

Fig. 16   Cologne, Collegiate Church of the Apostles, with former cloisters.

France from the early Romanesque period and from there it gradually spread by way of the Netherlands to the Rhine country.

The exterior of the east end of the Church of the Apostles is essentially Lower Rhenish in character. The apses are decorated with a double row of blind arcading and above these are a band of panelling and an eaves-gallery. These varied motifs are continued round the walls of the corner turrets imparting a sense of unity to the whole composition and emphasising the spatial character of this part of the church in contrast to the rest of the building. After the completion of the east end work was begun on the nave. Some of the 11th century piers and arcading still stood and a round-arched blind storey was added between these and the pointed clerestory windows. The roof was a sexpartite, ribbed cross vault while the side-aisles had groined cross vaults. Another master must have been responsible for the western choir, for it shows a much clearer understanding of the structural character of the embryonic Gothic style. Slender free-standing shafts shoot up from the pointed blind arcading or from the upper storey which is lit by much larger windows than the nave. This west end is indeed already Gothic.

pls. 184, 185   The sanctuary of St Maria im Kapitol, which was almost totally destroyed in the last war, was rebuilt in about 1200 on the plan of the Church of the Apostles, and the nave was given a sexpartite, ribbed cross vault in about 1240 also in the style of the neighbouring church.

pls. 186, 187   The former abbey church of St Martin, the most severely damaged of the Cologne churches in the last war, poses a number of interesting problems. It had belonged since the 10th century to an order of Scottish monks, but in the 12th century was inhabited by German Benedictines. It had an imposing trefoil east end with a massive tower over the choir and four slender corner turrets, two between the apses and two above the most easterly bays of the aisles. These latter were rebuilt in the 19th century after they had fallen in the years 1527 and 1789. The appearance of the tower, which formerly had a low roof instead of the later Rhenish spire, was unlike that of any other German church and owed its form to the same influence as the apses with their internal blind storeys. A tower exactly like it can be seen in *fig. 17* the Bayeux Tapestry in the representation of Westminster Abbey.

The general proportion of St Martin's revealed an increase in height which was

Fig. 17　From the Bayeux Tapestry: Edward the Confessor's burial
in Westminster Abbey.

indicative of the infiltration of the Gothic spirit. The height of the sanctuary was
emphasised by the use of pairs of very tall slender columns and by the articulation of
the lower storey with seven very narrow niches and numerous columns. This
sanctuary is similar in ground plan to that of the Church of the Apostles and there
is every reason to believe that St Martin's followed immediately on the former
church in date.

The rebuilding of the nave was begun as soon as the chancel was finished. It
consisted of only three bays with a very narrow western narthex. There was a
blind storey above the simple round-arched arcade and above that tall pointed
windows. Before the middle of the 13th century the nave was altered and a true
triforium took the place of the blind storey and pointed niches were introduced in
the upper walls to flank the windows. Though Gothic elements were present in this
Romanesque church the total impression was not of a Gothic structure.

A type of west end known in German as the *Westchorhalle*, in which the whole
structure is raised on a transept-shaped ground plan, occurs at Xanten. The twin- pls. 182, 183
towered west end as far as the third storey dates from 1190–1213. The upper stage
was added later and the lofty traceried windows are 16th century work. The oldest
part of the structure is decorated all over with shallow round-arched blind arcading,
which in the second storey frames the windows. The centre of the ground floor is
occupied by a recessed and pilastered, trefoil-headed portal. When the big Gothic

45

windows were put in, the centre bay of the interior was carried up to the height of the Gothic nave, but originally all three bays were the same height and their walls were divided into two stages by niches and blind arcading below and a gallery above.

The stylistic changes which were taking place towards the end of the 12th century are pre-eminently in evidence in the nave of St Castor's, Coblenz, which *pls. 130, 131* was rebuilt at that time. The chancel had already been redesigned in the middle of the century and terminated in an apse which was decorated externally with blind *fig. 18* arcading and an eaves-gallery. The nave was rebuilt on the old foundations and this accounts for the breadth of the main aisle. Four powerful shafts are attached to each of the rectangular piers and before the nave was vaulted in the late Gothic period these carried pointed wall arcading; and also served as supports for the round arches opening into the aisles. Between these arcade-arches and the clerestory

Fig. 18 Coblenz, former collegiate church of St Castor. Reconstruction of the interior as it looked towards the end of the 12th century.

windows the walls are pierced by pairs of arched openings forming a blind storey. This shows some attempt to articulate the walls, but it has no structural significance.

The sanctuary of the Cathedral at Trèves was rebuilt at the same time as the nave *pls. 114-123* of St Castor. It was begun under Archbishop Hillin (1152–69) but was only completed under Archbishop Johann in 1196. It takes the form of a square bay flanked *fig. 12* by towers and terminated by a five-sided apse. Five large, lofty windows illuminate this apse and above them are ranged pairs of small windows enclosed by arches. Vaulting shafts rise from both storeys to support eight powerful ribs which together with five longitudinal arches bear the weight of the semi-domical vault. The bay is roofed with a ribbed cross vault and its walls are richly articulated. On the ground floor there are openings into the towers and above them are two galleried storeys. All the arcade mouldings and the broad transverse arches are semicircular in section and many of them are ornamented with the pellet motif. The general effect, though not lacking in solemnity, is markedly decorative. There is no sign of that stress on verticality which makes St Martin's, Cologne so impressive. The exterior is principally remarkable for the buttresses at the corners of the polygonal apse, the disposition of which may have been inspired by examples in Lorraine.

It was only after a fire in the 18th century that the outer walls of the side aisles were built up higher than the vaulting and broken by windows to let more light into the nave. Despite all later additions and alterations the overwhelming sense of space experienced at Trèves is essentially due to the original basilican plan.

Shortly after the completion of the sanctuary at Trèves a new western choir was added to Mainz Cathedral. It was consecrated in 1239. The principal sanctuary was *pls. 90–99* already at the west end of Mainz and was accompanied by imposing transepts. It was otherwise a simple design and was now to be replaced by something truly monumental. The transepts were shortened and a massive tower was erected above the crossing, while the sanctuary was given the form of three polygonal apses flanked by slim corner turrets. The present arrangement of the various compartments in no way corresponds to the medieval aspect of the interior. The former sanctuary, which once contained the altar of St Martin and two side altars, is now filled with 18th century choir stalls, while the high altar stands in the crossing. The three apses open from huge, richly moulded piers at the corners of a square bay roofed with a domical ribbed cross vault. The apse vaults are carried on slender vaulting shafts rising the whole height of the walls, thus helping to create an impression of verticality. Externally an eaves-gallery runs round the three apses and they are surmounted by an attic storey, the gables of which display a profusion of ornament. The roof structure at Mainz is altogether full of variety and adds greatly to the picturesqueness of the group. The steeple of the octagonal crossing tower dates from 1767 and is the work of Franz Neumann, the son of the famous Balthasar. He was also responsible for the turret spires. Baroque, Gothic and Romanesque details are combined in a truly astonishing harmony in the exterior of Mainz, probably because in their later stages all styles are dominated by the tendency to become increasingly decorative.

Compared with that of Worms the west end of Mainz exhibits quite a different feeling for detail, yet both structures are the products of a late style, both set great store on picturesque grouping and both make use of forms found in French architecture while clinging to Rhenish traditions. In the Lower Rhineland, however, the borrowing of French forms resulted in a different type of architecture from that found along the Upper Rhine. Illuminating examples of the divergences are provided by the nave of the Abbey Church at Bonn, the trefoil plan of the convent church of St Quirin at Neuss and the central part of St Gereon at Cologne.

Towards the end of the 12th century the sanctuary at Bonn, which still had solid *pls. 144–151* walls pierced by tiny windows, was given a ribbed cross vault with pointed longitudinal and transverse arches. The vaulting shafts sprang from elaborately *fig. 19* carved corbels about six feet from the ground and a luxuriantly ornamented stringcourse marked the transition from wall to vault. The transepts were rebuilt at about the same time. Both terminated in polygonal apses and an octagonal tower was erected over the crossing. The walls of these transepts are solid except for the necessary openings to the aisles and the chambers on either side of the sanctuary. But the apses are richly articulated with blind arcading and with circular and round-headed windows and externally they are adorned with arcading and eaves-galleries.

The rebuilding of the nave at Bonn was entrusted to a master who had been trained in France and who made some radical changes. The piers and arcade-arches are entirely Romanesque in character but the upper part of the walls is enlivened by

48

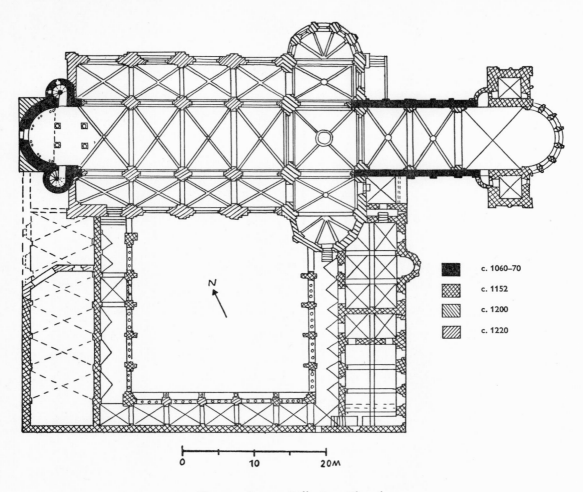

Fig. 19   Bonn, Collegiate Church.

c. 1060–70

c. 1152

c. 1200

c. 1220

0   10   20M

a true, round-arched triforium and above this is another gallery with round arches towards the nave corresponding windows in the outer wall. Externally these windows are framed by pointed blind arcading, while buttresses rise from the aisle walls to support the nave vault. The inspiration of this nave with its triforium and upper gallery is undeniably French, for triforia were not common in the Rhineland before the Gothic period.

Native tradition is, however, still manifest at Bonn in the capitals of the piers and in the round-arched arcade. It is details such as these which differentiate the abbey church at Bonn from the Cathedrals of Geneva and Lausanne which are similar in

49

structure but make use of early Gothic motifs. Probably all three buildings derive from French example. The date of the nave at Bonn is disputed, but the type of ornament used and the character of the round-arched arcade suggest that it was built under Prior Oliverius (1205–24).

The general form of this nave at Bonn is paralleled by that of the contemporary *pls. 166, 167* but more modest Benedictine church of Mönchen-Gladbach, and by that of the the infinitely more varied and more richly decorated convent church of St Quirinus at Neuss. The affinities between the late Romanesque and the Baroque styles in the *pls. 168, 169* Lower Rhineland are nowhere so clearly brought out as in this latter church. From the outside the majestic west end looks as though it had transepts, but inside there *fig. 20* are only very low compartments on either side of the central structure. Two flanking towers were originally planned instead of the present central tower. The aisled nave consists of three double bays and above the arcade are galleries with twin openings under pointed containing arches. These galleries and the one at the east end were used by the canonesses. The trefoil east end is exceedingly richly articulated and is certainly of later date than the nave. It includes the sanctuary and transepts and an octagonal tower over the crossing which is open to the church and

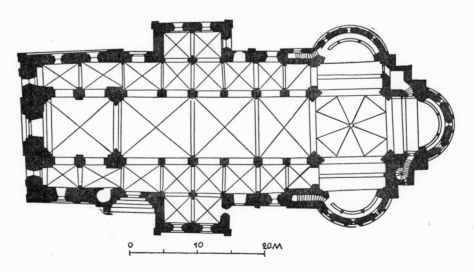

Fig. 20   Neuss, convent church of St Quirinus.

forms a lantern. The large crypt extends beneath the greater portion of this east end and necessitates a somewhat steep but picturesque ascent to the altar.

In comparison with other churches on the same plan as St Martin's and the Apostles at Cologne, St Quirinus exhibits a greater emphasis on verticality, not only in its proportions but in the formation of the piers and supports which are notably slender. While in the Cologne churches space is enclosed and the articulation of the walls enhances that enclosed effect, the object of the wall articulation at Neuss is to create a sensation of openness, even though this is counterbalanced to some extent by the heaviness of the walls behind the many free-standing pillars and the pointed arches of the east end.

The rebuilding of the Early Christian oval of St Gereon's, Cologne, which was *pls. 190, 191* begun in 1219 and finished in 1227, shows a great advance architecturally. The older building was made considerably higher. The lower niches were retained and above them was built a gallery of the same depth. The gallery openings occupy all the wall space between the vaulting shafts and are therefore structural and not merely ornamental. Above the gallery is a second very narrow gallery with fan-shaped windows, and the topmost, tallest storey contains yet a third gallery and lofty windows. Between these latter rise the supports of the domical roof. This structure is all arch and support and makes a strong impression of verticality.

The abbey church of St George at Limburg an der Lahn was rebuilt 1220–1235. It stands, like Durham, on a steep crag overlooking the river and dominating the *pls. 132–139* town. It is an outstanding example of that mingling of the round and pointed arch to which Rhenish Germany clung with such tenacity long after the disappearance of the former from the architecture of other localities and countries. The monumental character of the west front derives from the two massive, square, five-storeyed towers which look as though they were constructed of great blocks placed one upon another with neither buttresses nor shafts to connect them and stress their verticality. Above the crossing at the east end there is an octagonal tower crowned with a spire, and slender corner towers flank both the north and south transepts, so that altogether this majestic church boasts no less than seven towers.

The aspect of the aisled nave is most imposing. It is divided into two great rectangular bays roofed with sexpartite vaulting, while the broad aisles are covered with groined vaults. The nave piers are plain and sturdy, but the slender shafts supporting the ribs are arranged in graceful clusters with foliated capitals. The apsidal sanctuary is not very large and round it runs a processional aisle with chapels scooped out of the thickness of the walls. The elevations of nave, choir and transepts are divided into four stages by arches, triforium, secondary gallery and clerestory. This arrangement has much in common with that of North eastern French churches like Laon and Noyon. St George's, Limburg possesses a feature which may have been directly borrowed from one of these French churches: a triforium which completely encircles the interior. In the nave each arch of this triforium contains two pointed openings. In the transepts and choir these openings are tripartite, the central one, much stilted, almost touching the containing arch. The use to which the galleries were put is not definitely known. As they do not occur in the more considerable churches of the same district it is to be supposed that they were not introduced as merely ornamental features but because more space was needed. It appears that both nave and transepts were open to the people.

The first genuinely Gothic church to be built in the Rhineland was the Liebfrauen-kirche at Trèves which was begun in 1235 and completed in about 1253. It stands pls. 124, 125 to the south of the Cathedral and replaces the southern of the two original Early Christian churches. The ground plan is polygonal with the sanctuary projecting fig. 21 from it, but the superstructure is cruciform and crowned by a tower. About a central square are ranged two square bays to north, south and west terminating in half-hexagonal apses, while to the east an additional bay forms the sanctuary with

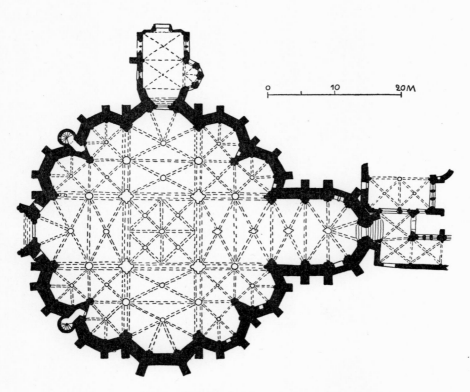

Fig. 21   Trèves, Church of Our Lady (Liebfrauenkirche).

its polygonal apse. Square bays occur between the arms of the cross, each opening into two half-hexagonal chapels, which together with the apses of the cross make up the polygonal ground plan. The main door is in the western apse. There is no earlier example of a plan such as this in the Rhineland, for the octagons at Aix-la-Chapelle and Ottmarsheim cannot be compared with it. The elevation of the central cross is two-storeyed and the lower storey is taller than the upper, which helps to create that overwhelming sense of verticality which is so essentially Gothic. The piers at the corners of the crossing take the form common in French cathedrals. They consist of cylindrical columns with four attached shafts and fine foliated capitals; the corner piers of the apses are more richly articulated and are informed with a soaring, dynamic quality, while the piers of the central compartment are slim, cylindrical and without shafts, and the elaborately moulded, pointed arches they support seem to shoot up from them like rays of light. The apse windows are partly blind, but these compartments are dominated like the whole building with the fugue-like rhythm of pillar and arch. Processional aisles encircle the apses on both floors. In the sanctuary apse all the windows are fully lighted so that the impact of the stained glass, which once filled them, was instantly felt by the faithful as they entered by the west door. Despite its picturesque character every component of this lofty interior has structural significance.

Externally the cruciform shape with its central tower stands out from the cluster of corner chapels with their small round turrets; and the powerful buttresses and lofty traceried windows re-echo the theme of the interior. The west front wears a more solid aspect. The sculptured portal is the first of its kind in the Rhineland and is treated in the French manner. The gable is surmounted by a magnificent Crucifixion, but the larger figures are not the originals, which were savaged during the French Revolution. The reliefs in the tympanum showing the Virgin Enthroned, the Angel announcing the Virgin Birth to the Shepherds, The Adoration of the Kings, The Presentation in the Temple and the Massacre of the Innocents are all original, as are some of the figures in the six archivolts, the angels, popes, bishops and the wise and foolish virgins. There are other portals on the north and east sides of the church but only the east portal is decorated with sculpture. There is a relief of the Coronation of the Virgin in the tympanum.

The Cathedral at Trèves remained as it was left in the late Romanesque period. At Cologne, however, it was decided that the old, much altered Carolingian church should be replaced by a new and handsome building in the French style. There were several reasons for this. Firstly the Archbishop as a political opponent of the Hohenstauffen wished to emphasise his importance; secondly a new church was necessary to symbolise the prominence of Cologne as a flourishing centre of commerce, and finally the old building was considered inadequate to house the famous relics, the bones of the Three Kings which Frederick Barbarossa had captured at the siege of Milan nearly a century before. So when the Cathedral caught fire in 1248 it was allowed to burn down and in August of the same year the foundation stone of the new church was laid by Archbishop Conrad of Hochstaden. The work was entrusted to one, Master Gerard, who is mentioned in the records as

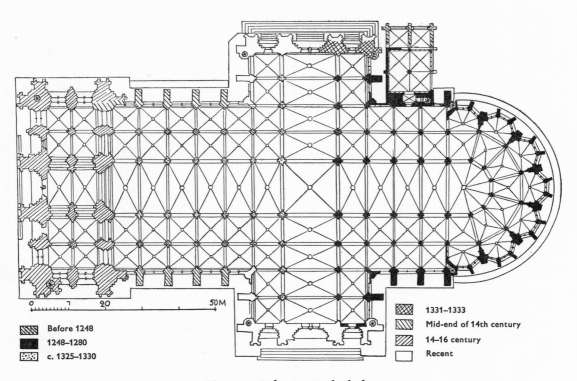

Fig. 22   Cologne, Cathedral.

55

pls. 192–200

fig. 22

"iniciator" and "rector fabricae". All the essential features of the plan were devised by him. He began with the chancel. In French Gothic cathedrals the choir and sanctuary formed one long compartment which terminated in a processional aisle with a corona of chapels. Before he was summoned to Cologne, Master Gerard had worked on the Cathedral of Amiens, and this was clearly his model for the Rhenish church. The chancel at Cologne is aisled and consists of four square bays ending in a seven-sided apse encircled by a processional aisle and a corona of seven chapels. The nave at Cologne is shorter than that at Amiens and the arrangement of the towers at the west end is different. At Amiens the towers have literally no ground floor compartments while at Cologne four bays occupy the base of each tower.

When the choir at Cologne was begun the nave at Amiens was already completed, but the only parts of the chancel to have been finished were the processional aisle and the chapels. The work then came to a standstill and was only continued after a fire in 1258. Master Gerard therefore could only have known the lower part of the chancel and his plans for the rest of the structure at Cologne were entirely his own. He himself only saw the completion of the first stages of the chancel for by 1279 he was dead. His successors were Master Arnold and, after 1308, Arnold's son Johann. The chancel was finally consecrated in 1322.

The interior of the chancel is dominated by the tremendous height of the central aisle which rises to a height of about 150 feet and is nearly 50 feet wide. The lofty pointed arches of the arcade, the large triforium openings and clerestory windows, the clustered columns and the remarkable tall slender lancets of the apse all contribute to the impression of soaring weightlessness, the negation of wall space achieved by a composition of pillars and arches. At Amiens a horizontal band carved with foliage runs below the triforium passing over the shafts; at Cologne there is a similar horizontal band, but the vaulting shafts interrupt it in a conscious attempt to achieve verticality. The tracery of triforium, chapels and sanctuary has French parallels at Amiens and St Denis.

The profusion of sculpture at Cologne is specially remarkable. Each of the fourteen piers of the chancel is adorned by a splendid figure on a foliated corbel; on the north side stands Christ, on the south the Virgin, each accompanied by six apostles. Above each of these statues is a lofty pinnacled canopy. It is possible that the sculptor responsible for them had seen the similar figures of the Apostles in the Sainte Chapelle at Paris, which was completed in 1248.

The five-aisled nave is a typical Lower Rhenish design, and the richly varied forms of the buttresses above the side aisles and chapels, especially the lavishly ornamented flying buttresses, are also in the local tradition. While the chapel buttresses, which were constructed by Master Gerard, are relatively simple, those over the side aisles are cruciform in shape and abundantly decorated with tracery and every variety of pinacle giving the impression that the chancel is embedded in a petrified thicket. The multitude of soaring pointed members is swelled by steep gables rising above the intricate parapet.

After the completion of the chancel, work on the Cathedral progressed very slowly and finally in 1560 it was abandoned altogether. In 1325 the south aisles were still incomplete, but the two northern aisles were finished before the end of the 14th century and the stained glass was added early in the 16th century. The broad, majestic west end was begun in 1350 and the work was continued from 1353 until 1390 under Master Michael of Savoy. The northern tower was only carried up to the height of the aisles, but the southern tower was built up as far as the third storey so that in 1437 the bells could be hung, yet it was not fully completed until 1868. During the Romantic period some of the original plans were discovered and there were many enthusiasts who were eager to resume the work so laid aside. Finally in 1842 King Frederick William IV laid the foundation stone for the last stage of the work and it was eventually brought to a conclusion in 1880. The Cathedral was damaged in the last war but has already been almost entirely restored. The 19th century builders closely followed the style of the chancel. Their five-aisled nave is of immense breadth but so lofty is the central aisle that the effect is one of surging verticality. The Gothic conception of space is most clearly embodied in this structure: the perspective leads the eye irresistably towards the sanctuary, while at the same time the steep ascent of all the forms encourages the contemplation of infinity. The west end with its two great towers was carried out in strict accordance with the original plans even although it was found that the part which had been built in the Middle Ages deviated from these plans in some respects. The elevation of the west front is quite different from that of French cathedrals. The treatment is linear rather than plastic. The buttresses, though structurally necessary, appear decorative rather than functional. The portals and windows are so lavishly ornamented that the whole of the lower part of the structure seems to be covered with a network of linear patterns divided into stages by horizontal string-courses, yet predominantly vertical. The decoration of the upper parts of the towers and their spires reinforces this impression of linear design. Of the three west portals only the unusually narrow south door is medieval and only five of the statues are old, the Apostles Peter, Andrew and James on the left and St Paul and St John on the right, which all date from 1375.

pls. 166, 167   According to documentary evidence Master Gerard of Cologne was also responsible for the new chancel of the church at Mönchen-Gladbach, which was consecrated in 1275. It resembles that at Cologne except that it has no processional aisle.

pls. 36–45   While plans for the rebuilding of Cologne were going forward the nave of Strassburg was gothicised. During the 13th century many of the German bishoprics *fig. 9*   tried to become independent. In Cologne, for instance, Archbishop Siegfried of Westerburg was forced by the citizens to give up his rights and move his see to Bonn. The citizens of Strassburg had already gained their freedom in 1262 after their victory over Bishop Walther von Geroldseck at the Battle of Oberhausbergen. The inhabitants of Cologne, however, where there were many fine churches, took little interest in the building of the Cathedral, and left all the arrangements to the Dean and Chapter. But at Strassburg the Cathedral was regarded as a monument to the independence of the citizens and they took over the administration of the building operations and after 1395 bore the whole burden of expenses. Their interest naturally centred in that part of the Cathedral which had always been open to them, namely the nave and the west end, which was to tower above the Rhine as a symbol of their civic pride. The attitude of the people of Strassburg towards their Cathedral is typical of that of many medieval communities. The magnificence of numbers of English parish churches is due to the desire of lay individuals to erect a monument to their own importance as well as to the glory of God, and in Germany the present Cathedral at Freiburg was originally a parish church built at the expense of the townsfolk; and there, as in England, citizens were responsible for the founding of countless sumptuous chapels.

58

The rebuilding of the nave at Strassburg was probably begun shortly before the middle of the 13th century. The work made rapid progress and by 1275 the vault was in place. A certain Master Rudolf is thought to have been the architect. He built over the foundations of the old 11th century structure and this explains the unusual breadth of the main aisle. The articulation of the walls is altogether French in spirit. The piers are not quite so tall as was usual at that period but are furnished with as many as sixteen attached shafts. Above the arcade runs a triforium with traceried openings and the whole nave exhibits that intense delight in lavish ornament which is more characteristic of the Lower than the Upper Rhine. The details here have much in common with forms which occur at St Denis. A charming testimony to the part played by the citizens in the building and furnishing of the Cathdral is provided by the stained glass in the north aisle. It depicts all the German kings and emperors in token of the townspeople's gratitude for their deliverance from the rule of the bishops. The stained glass in the south aisle and the clerestory shows figures of the saints and scenes from the lives of Christ and the Virgin. The fresco of the Last Judgment over the crossing arch is a 19th century work by Ludwig Steinheil. Chapels were added in the 14th and 16th centuries and placed in the corners between nave and transepts.

Externally the nave shows great individuality. The buttresses are without the variety of those at Cologne and are only enlivened by small animal and grotesque sculptures. They are extremely heavy and insist on form rather than ornament. The broad, powerful flying buttresses are pierced by quatrefoil openings, such as do not occur in France. Master Rudolf must certainly have known a good deal about French architecture but his own work is entirely original.

The chief pride of Strassburg is the west front. A painted inscription on the main portal, which is no longer legible, stated that the work was begun by Master Erwin von Steinbach in 1277. The Romanesque foundations were widened so that the facade is broader than the nave and the towers project beyond the aisles. The wall connecting the towers is the same width as the main aisle and is distinguished by powerful buttresses, a recessed portal and a great rose window. The peculiarity of this west front is that it is conceived as an independent composition. The two lower stages are decorated with unusual free-standing slender shafts, the vertical lines of which are interrupted by the steep openwork gables of the three sculptured portals. The large rose window is set back in a square framework of tracery. This window, the design of the gables and the style of the canopied figures on the buttresses all have their counterparts in French architecture, but the treatment of the towers is decidedly Rhenish. These richly decorated, but extremely solid blocks of masonry have none of the character of the openwork towers of Reims and St Nicaise. They were only carried up as far as the first storey by the time of Erwin's death in 1318 and the work was completed by Masters Johann and Gerlach. It was not until the end of the 14th century that it was decided to increase the height of the towers in accordance with the original plan, and then only the north tower received attention. An octagonal stage was added to it by Ulrich von Ensingen (1399–1419) and over this Johann Hültz of Cologne raised the glittering openwork spire, a typical late Gothic work, built 1420–39. The sculpture on the three portals is only partly original as a great deal of the work was destroyed during the French Revolution, but the willowy figures and fluted draperies of the wise and foolish virgins show Gothic sculpture at its best.

pls. 52–63 Strassburg Cathedral was a potent influence in the valley of the Upper Rhine and this is nowhere more clearly seen than at Freiburg im Breisgau, where the parish church was only raised to the rank of a cathedral in 1827. The transepts and the great part of the two little eastern towers date from the late Romanesque period. The master responsible for the gothicising of the original Romanesque nave was not entirely at ease in the new style; the window tracery at the east end of the south is noticeably unwieldy and there are large areas of solid wall in the clerestory. There is no triforium to break the monotony of the walls above the arcade, though the piers have attached columns like those at Strassburg and a gallery enlivens the outer walls of the aisles. This latter motif, which does not occur at Strassburg, is found in Burgundy and derives from Norman example.

When the two most easterly of the four nave bays were completed a more progressive master took over the work. The most remarkable features of his achievement are the ornamentation of the blind arcading in the aisles and the arrangement of the rose windows in the west walls of the aisles. They are placed not in the centre but on the outer edges of the walls.

60

The most celebrated feature of Freiburg Cathedral is, however, the west tower. The two lower stages were the work of Master Gerhart and were finished by 1301. The stately porch is surmounted by a gable containing a relief of the Coronation of the Virgin and the richly moulded inner portal is abundantly decorated with French inspired sculpture. Above the porch is the Chapel of St Michael which opens into the nave, and externally the porch is flanked by powerful buttresses which dominate the lower part of the tower.

The upper part of the tower was built between 1310 and 1350. Above the clock is a low projecting, twelve-cornered parapet which encircles the lofty openwork octagonal base of the lace-like spire. This is the oldest Gothic tower in the Rhineland and it served as a model for many others although the only tower in the region which bears any marked resemblance to it is that on the north side of the chancel of the abbey church of St Theobald at Thann, which was built during the second half of the 14th century. The master mason of this filigree spire was Remigius Faesch of Basle.

Shortly after the completion of the west tower the citizens of Freiburg set about rebuilding the east end, where the most prominent families and the guilds were anxious to establish chapels for themselves. A large chancel was necessary to accommodate all the clergy officiating in these chapels, and the completed east end consisted of a long compartment with a processional aisle and a chevet of thirteen chapels. The foundation stone was laid in 1354 and the plan was probably by Johann von Gmünd. Work on the building came to a standstill owing to lack of resources and the chancel was not finally consecrated until 1513. It is a typical late Gothic work enlivened with flamboyant tracery, lierne vaults, and richly ornamented buttresses. The spires of the two east towers are miniature replicas of the west spire.

The design of the abbey church of St Martin at Kolmar (rebuilt from 1263) shows how strongly the Upper Rhineland resisted the full implications of the Gothic *pls. 32–34* style despite the adoption of tracery, buttresses and Gothic ornament. The triple-aisled basilica consists of five bays; and the rather short, massive piers are cylindrical with four powerful attached shafts. The walls are solid-looking and there is no triforium. The same impression of mass is inspired by the chancel which was built in the 14th century, for it is only in the three-sided apse where pointed arches lead into the surrounding chapels that the wall space is seriously interrupted. The vaulting shafts between the narrow windows are not organic parts of the structure as in true Gothic.

pls. 48–51   The convent church of St Stephen at Breisach on the right bank of the Rhine was rebuilt in about 1300. The original late Romanesque church had a broad, but short and rather low nave with a ribbed cross vault, transepts with two eastern apses and two towers flanking the sanctuary. It makes an impression of heaviness despite the introduction of pointed arches and Gothic vaults. Owing to the position of the church on an incline the new sanctuary needed a substructure and this took the form of an octagonal chapel with a central pier. Externally the new east end is very solid-looking, for the windows are narrow and the buttresses are not truly structural. The same is true of the south tower. The whole exterior, indeed, has a massive, weighty appearance, so that if it were not for the Gothic design of the windows the church could easily be taken for a late Romanesque work.

Further characteristic examples of this adherence to a static conception of architecture combined with the adoption of Gothic detail are to be found in the nave of the Benedictine church of St Peter and St Paul at Weissenburg and in the Premonstratensian church of St Nicholas at Hagenau.

The idea of erecting a single tower above a broad west end was realised at Strassburg in the church of the Scottish monastery of St Thomas, the plan of which dates from the first half of the 13th century. It is a massive structure which has no stylistic affinities with the tower at Freiburg. The chief interest of St Thomas' resides, however, not in the tower but in the nave which was designed by Master Johann Erlin in about 1330 and consists of three aisles of equal height. This is the only "hall" church on the Upper Rhine.

pls. 46, 47

fig. 23

The traditional differences between the architecture of the Upper and Lower Rhineland is sufficiently in evidence in the churches of the Romanesque period, but it is still more strongly marked in the works of the Gothic age. While in the Upper Rhineland none of the abbey churches has a triforium and the walls of all tend to look solid, the larger Gothic churches of the Lower Rhine illustrate the constructive principles of true Gothic whereby the building consists of a skeleton

62

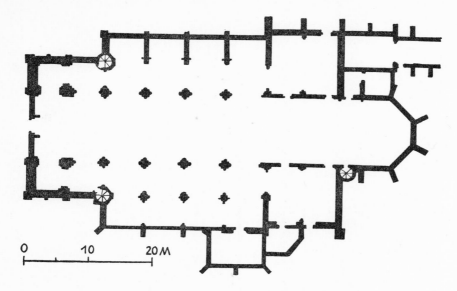

Fig. 23   Strassburg, Monastic Church of St Thomas.

of piers, buttresses, arches and ribbed vaulting. A fine example of this style is
provided by the church of the Cistercian monastery at Altenberg, which replaced *pls. 178–181*
a Romanesque building in 1255. The plan includes a five-aisled chancel with a
seven-sided apse and a chevet of seven chapels; transepts with the choir in the *fig. 24*
crossing and the so-called "ducal choir" in the north transept, (in which were situated
the tombs of the founder, Count von Berg, and his family); and an aisled nave. The
sanctuary with its ten altars was built with all possible speed and consecrated in 1287.
The transepts were finished by 1300, but work on the nave was protracted until
after 1379. Master Walther was responsible for the design, but he died in 1270 and
the work was continued by Master Reynold whose tombstone in the nave cele-
brates him as "super omnes rex lapicidas".

The Gothic motifs in this church are all used structurally. There is a triforium
above the pointed, moulded arcade-arches and above it, separated from it only by a
narrow horizontal band, the large clerestory windows occupy the entire space
between the vaulting shafts. The capitals in the chancel are sparsely decorated with
leaf ornaments. The plan of the sanctuary resembles those of many French Cistercian churches, particularly Longpont (1227) and Royaumont (1235). The exterior

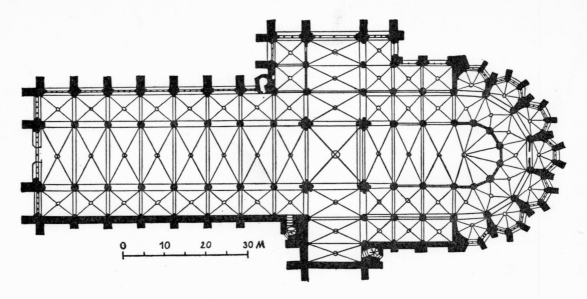

Fig. 24   Altenberg, Cistercian church.

is rather severe, for the buttresses are simple, and there is no tower and no sculptural decoration except an enchanting little group of the Annunciation over the west door, dating from 1375.

pls. 182, 183 Lower Rhenish characteristics are revealed with peculiar clarity by the monastic church of Xanten, which was damaged in the last war. The chancel was rebuilt 1263–1437, while the west end was only finished in 1559. The nave is five-aisled, there are no transepts and the east end is similar to that of the Liebfrauenkirche at Trèves. The whole structure is emphatically based on a system of arch and support. But the desire to replace solid walls by large stained glass windows and attenuated supports is most fully realised in the choir and sanctuary of the chapel at Aix-la-Chapelle which was rebuilt between 1355 and 1414 owing to the growing *pls. 158–163* importance of the building as the place of coronation of the Holy Roman Emperors. *fig. 3* The entire wall space between the vaulting shafts is occupied by windows.

In the region of the Lower Rhine which is adjacent to the Netherlands the Gothic style was inhibited in its development. "Hall" churches are rare, the oldest example *pls. 174, 175* being the convent church of Essen, which was built in about 1275 to replace a 9th century foundation. Nave and aisles are of the same height and consist of four bays.

The piers are simple cylinders and narrow galleries run along the aisle walls behind the vaulting shafts. The sanctuary above the old crypt is square-ended and like the nave has no clerestory.

Later 14th century "hall" churches include the Dominican foundation at Aix-la-Chapelle and the convent church of St Lambert at Düsseldorf. The church of the Holy Ghost at Heidelberg with its stately "hall" choir dates from the 15th century. The "hall" church of Cleves (1341–1426) merits a more detailed mention. The *fig. 25* pentagonal east end with its tall, slender, traceried windows is flanked by polygonal chapels. The choir is separated from the nave by a rood screen and takes in two of the rectangular bays of the main aisle. The cylindrical piers with their four attached shafts support perfectly plain pointed arches and above them are broad, blind traceried windows. The only light in the nave comes from the side aisles and from the large west window. The west end is graced by two proud, buttressed towers and below the west window is a lofty portal. This church is built mainly of brick, stone only being used for the piers, arches and the sculpture on the portal.

The convent church of Our Lady at Oberwesel between Coblenz and Bingen is surprisingly heavy in character, perhaps partly on account of the material in which *pls. 106–108*

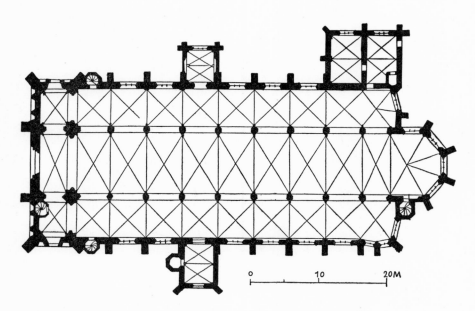

Fig. 25   Cleves, Collegiate Church.

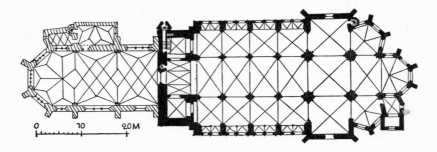

Fig. 26 Oppenheim, St Catherine's.

it is built, slate. The five-sided apse with its tall slender traceried windows has, it is true, a narrow recessed passage above the first storey, but in the nave an almost unbroken wall rises above the massive hexagonal piers and the low arcade-arches. The external walls are also without articulation and the west end is crowned by a formidable square tower with a low octagonal superstructure.

pls. 101–105 The convent church of St Catherine at Oppenheim affords a striking contrast to the building at Oberwesel. It was erected between 1262 and 1370 and is astonishingly fig. 26 richly articulated. The ground plan of the sanctuary resembles that of the convent church at Cleves except that it has projecting transepts the gable ends of which were profusely decorated with openwork in the 14th century, when the majestic octagonal tower over the crossing was provided with a steeple. The nave is aisled, numerous shafts, separated by deep fillets, cluster about the piers, and there is no triforium but four-light, traceried windows open immediately above the arcading. In each of the aisle bays, between the buttresses, are low chapels above the entrances to which rise broad, richly traceried windows. The church stands on a hill from the foot of which the south side looks like a facade. For that very reason the tracery on this side is particularly elaborately patterned and the buttresses and gables are encrusted with a superfluity of ornament. Between 1415 and 1439 an immense choir with a five-sided apse and huge traceried windows was built by Madern Gertener to project beyond the west towers. This double choir arrangement is unusual in a Gothic church.

The predilection for more decorative forms which is so strikingly manifest at Oppenheim and which we have seen to be typical of the Lower rather than the Upper

66

Rhine makes itself felt in many of the late Gothic Upper Rhenish works. Oppenheim has indeed certain affinities with Upper Rhenish architecture and because of this and because of its geographical position it provides a link between the churches of the Upper and Lower Rhine. During the late Gothic period there was some exchange of ideas between the two regions. As we have seen, a master from Cologne was appointed to complete the tower of Strassburg, and architects from the Parler family worked in Cologne as well as in Freiburg and Basle. In comparison with the rest of Germany both parts of the Rhineland seem to be of equal importance stylistically, for it was through their example that the Gothic manner was transmitted to neighbouring territories. But while most Gothic churches in Germany were of the "hall" type, the Rhenish architects with few exceptions remained faithful to the basilican tradition.

THE BAROQUE PERIOD

The few churches built in the Rhineland after the close of the Gothic era drew their inspiration from southern Germany or from Italy. No new churches were built on the Rhine during the Renaissance period and the only important Baroque foundations were the churches of the Jesuits. It is a singular fact that the Jesuit buildings in the Rhineland were at first all dominated by the Gothic style. The two most important churches are those at Molsheim in Alsace and at Cologne, both *pl. 35* designed by Christoph Wamser. The church at Molsheim (1615–18) is a triple-aisled basilica with galleries and low transepts with a small porch on the north side and a sacristy on the south, and with polygonal apses to the east. The chancel terminates in a three-sided apse. With its lofty traceried window this east end is definitely Gothic in character and like the nave is roofed with lierne vaults while the galleries and aisles are ceiled with ribbed cross vaults. The extraordinary breadth of the nave is, however, alien to the Gothic spirit, and the pointed arcade-arches rest on Doric columns.

fig. 27 The Jesuit church of the Assumption at Cologne (1618–27) is similar in plan but much more ostentatious. The nave is again very broad, but has more height and the piers with their Tuscan capitals are much taller than those as Molsheim. The aisles and galleries are roofed with stellar vaults. The chancel is close to that of Molsheim; it has the same lofty traceried windows and powerful buttresses. The decorative figures of the Apostles on the buttresses are the work of a south German sculptor from Augsburg, Jeremias Geisselbrunn. The tall facade flanked by towers, shows the same combination of Gothic and classical forms as the interior. The large west window is filled with Gothic tracery, while the portal beneath it boasts Corinthian columns, and the tower at the east end displays Romanesque and Gothic detail though it is crowned with a Baroque lantern and cupola.

The Church of St Andrew at Düsseldorf, built only a few years later, is entirely

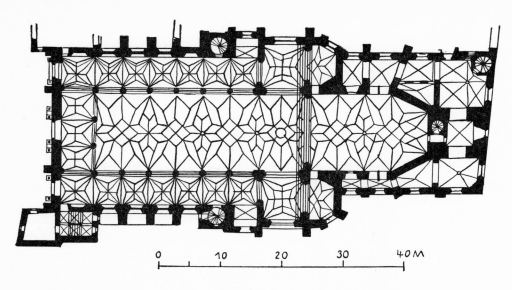

Fig. 27   Cologne, Jesuit Church of the Assumption.

in the Italo-German Baroque style. The nave is of the "hall" type, the piers are furnished with fluted Corinthian shafts and support round arches and the building is roofed with plaster cross vaults with broad ribs and elaborate stucco bosses. The chancel is flanked by two stately towers and terminates in a three-sided sanctuary. Behind the high altar a passage leads to the domed mausoleum of the Dukes of Pfalz-Neuburg, one of whom founded the church. The exterior of the church is articulated by columns and elaborate string-courses and the facade is pedimented in the Italian manner. But despite its pronounced Baroque character, this building clings to the medieval traditions of South Germany in its retention of the "hall" plan.

The Jesuit church at Heidelberg, which was begun by Johann Adam Breunig in 1712, is conceived as a pure "hall" design without galleries. It has powerful clustered *pls. 65, 66* piers, round arches and a cross groined vault, and chapels open from the north and south aisles between the buttresses.

The Jesuit church at Mannheim (1733–1760) is more like the Baroque churches of south Germany. The North Italian architect Alessandro Galli da Bibiena was *fig. 28* responsible for the plan, but he died in 1748 and Franz Wilhelm Rabaliatti worked on the building until 1754. The illusionist ceiling frescoes and the wealth of stucco-work were executed under Peter Anton Verschaffelt by Egid Quirid Asam and his assistants. The most effective part of this handsome church is the cupola which is lit by an octagonal lantern and fantastically decorated. The sanctuary is apsidal and round-headed windows illuminate the splendid pilastered and sculptured high altar making it the focus of the whole dazzling composition. In all Gothic cathedrals and abbey churches the chancel was separated from the nave by a rood screen. This screen was largely abandoned in the Baroque period and the whole design centred dramatically about the high altar.

Externally the church at Mannheim is rectangular in the lower storeys, narrowing as it rises and flaunting a cupola above the transept gables. The west pediment is flanked by onion-domed towers and the whole facade is enriched with pilasters, diverse window openings, balusters, blind arcading and statues in niches. The porch pediment displays a dynamic relief of Christ's monogram and adoring angels.

pls. 126–129 The Jesuit church of St Paulinus at Trèves had been destroyed by the French in 1674 and the Elector Archbishop Franz Georg von Schönborn commissioned the celebrated Johann Balthasar Neumann to draw up plans for a new building. The foundation stone was laid in 1734 and the church was consecrated in 1757. The Trèves architect Josef Walter was in charge of the building operations until 1744 when the work was taken over by Neumann's pupil Johannes Seitz. Externally it is an aisleless structure with an apsidal chancel and a lanterned tower rising above the pilastered porch of the undulating west end. The interior is, by contrast, astonishingly ostentatious and articulated in a most original manner. The tall, round-

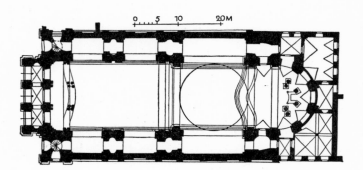

Fig. 28   Mannheim, Jesuit Church.

headed windows are recessed between engaged, compound piers with massive jutting imposts so that the broken wall surfaces seem to be instinct with movement. The vault is decorated with frescoes by the Augsburg painter Thomas Scheffler and the splendour of the interior is enhanced by a profusion of stucco ornament, by the incredible richness of the pilastered altar with its tall baldachin and the wrought iron screen above the flight of steps leading up to the chancel. Yet it is a decorative rather than a structural composition for the great piers do not support an entablature as in Italian churches.

This type of church was by no means general in the Rhineland. Even in the second half of the 18th century "hall" churches were still being built there and of these the abbey church of St Peter at Mainz is an enchanting example. The main aisle is nearly three times as broad as the side aisles and immense windows cast a brilliant light on the ravishing Rococo decoration.

Many abbey churches of the Baroque period are externally very simple but overwhelmingly ornate inside. Even small churches built at this time combine a remarkable sense of space organisation with delight in sumptuous decoration. Such is the *pl. 64* Dominican foundation of St Katharinenthal near Diessenhofen in Switzerland on the left bank of the Rhine between Stein and Schaffhausen. It was the work of Johann Michael Beer in 1732-35. The broad nave consists of only two almost square bays vaulted with richly painted and stuccoed saucer domes supported by commanding piers. To the east there are side altars, to the west a gallery, and the saucer-domed chancel is flanked by chapels. The nuns' choir is situated behind the opulent high altar so that the sisters were hidden from the gaze of the people; the nuns conducted their private devotions in the west gallery where they were protected by a balustrade and a wrought iron screen.

One of the more interesting facts to emerge from this brief study of the more important Rhineland churches is perhaps that the majority exhibit the characteristics of the later developments of the styles in which they are built and show a marked inclination for rich decorative effects. This is apparent in the Gothic cathedrals of Strassburg and Cologne and is generally only suppressed when the rule of an Order such as the Cistercian or the Minorite insists on austerity. Nevertheless the distinc-

71

tion between the Upper and Lower Rhenish conceptions of architecture is maintained throughout the periods under survey. With few exceptions the architects of the Upper Rhine remain faithful to the tradition of articulating space by means of enclosed units.

CHURCHES MENTIONED AND ILLUSTRATED

AIX-LA-CHAPELLE, former Palatine Chapel, page 13, 64, plates 158–163, fig. 3.

Charlemagne's Imperial palace stood on the site of the present town-hall north of the Chapel. The latter was at the same time a collegiate church and from 813 to 1531 German kings were crowned in it. In 1801, under French rule, the See of Aix-la-Chapelle was founded and the collegiate church became a cathedral. The See was abolished in 1821 but revived in 1930.

ALTENBERG, Cistercian Church, page 63, plates 178–181, fig. 24.

Count Adolph I von Berg donated in 1133 his family castle to the Cistercian monastery of Morimond. The first church, begun in 1135 and completed in 1160 (choir consecrated in 1145) was built according to Cistercian custom in the valley at the foot of the hill on which stood the castle. The monastery was abolished in 1803; rebuilding began in 1835, and by 1857 the edifice was again in use as a non-denominational parish church. The flying buttresses supporting the nave are a 19th century addition; originally there were only simple triangular buttressing walls. The former monastic buildings stood on the south side, the south transept being accordingly smaller. Last restoration in 1908–10. The Annunciation group on the West front is a copy; original now inside.

BASLE, Minster, page 24, 39, plates 24, 25, fig. 15.

Remains of foundation walls of a Carolingo-Ottonian structure in the form of a semicircular enclosed sanctuary with two corresponding chapels have been excavated in the territory of the former palace east of the present sanctuary.

BONN, Collegiate Church, page 48, plates 144–151, fig. 19.

Stands on the site of a Late Roman burial place; a small church was built in the 4th century and extended in the Carolingian period. Of the large 11th century structure there survive parts of the crypt, the lower walls of the choir as well as the foundations of the west apse which is flanked by two round towers. The late Romanesque church, many times restored, was heavily damaged in the last war but has since been in all essentials faithfully rebuilt.

BRAUWEILER, Benedictine Monastery Church, page 35, plates 164, 165.

Nothing survives of the first church founded in 1024; of the early Romanesque structure, raised in 1048–61, the crypt and parts of the transept have been preserved. Of the 12th century abbey buildings there survive the cloister court, the Medardus Chapel and the interior of the chapter house with extensive wall-paintings dating from about 1174.

BREISACH, Collegiate Church of St Stephen, page 62, plates 48–51.

CLEVES, Collegiate Church, page 65, fig. 25.

COBLENZ, Collegiate Church of St Castor, page 17, 46, plates 130, 131, fig. 18.

COLOGNE, Cathedral, page 11, 14, 55, plates 192–200, fig. 22.

COLOGNE, Collegiate Church of the Apostles, page 42, plate 188, fig. 16.

COLOGNE, Convent Church of St Ursula, page 36.

COLOGNE, Great St Martin's, page 44, plates 186, 187, fig. 17.

COLOGNE, Jesuit Church of the Assumption, page 68, fig. 27.

COLOGNE, St George, page 31.

COLOGNE, St Gereon's, page 11, 38, 51, plates 190, 191, fig. 2.

COLOGNE, St Maria im Kapitol, page 31, 44, plates 184, 185.

COLOGNE, St Pantaleon's, page 20, plate 189, fig. 7.

CONSTANCE, Minster, page 24, plates 18–23.

The rebuilding, with alterations, of the Romanesque church began after the fire in 1299 with a new roofing and the replacement of the Romanesque crossing-tower (remains survive) by a Gothic turret; the present one dates from 1566. South-west tower rebuilt in 1378, after the earthquake of 1356. Vaulting began in 1430, first the choir, then the sanctuary, the transept wings and the aisles; in the nave it was left unfinished; the present nave vault dates from 1680.

The architect in charge was from 1453 Vincenz Ensinger, from 1490 Lucas Böblinger. Chapels were added to the sides of the aisles, and the transept façades were also given a Gothic appearance. In the north arm of the transept, the so-called *Thomas Choir*, an open tower called *Schnegg,* was erected in 1438 by Master Antoni—a curiously ornate structure giving access to the vault. A Gothic west front appeared between 1497–1511; after a fire in 1511 the upper storeys were rebuilt in 1515–24; their present form with the central tower structure dates from the restoration of 1844–60.

DÜSSELDORF, Church of St Andrew, page 68.

DÜSSELDORF, Collegiate Church of St Lambert, page 65.
   The present structure dates from the end of the 13th century; enlarged in 1370–94. Three-aisled hall church, brick partly faced with tufa; the sanctuary is closed on five sides with an ambulatory running on from the aisles. In front of the façade, west tower (spire in 1815). Considerably damaged in the last war, now fully rebuilt.

EBERBACH, Cistercian Monastery, page 35, plates 109–113.

ESSEN, Ladies' Collegiate Church, page 21, 64, plates 174, 175.

FREIBURG IM BREISGAU, Cathedral, page 60, plates 52–63.

HAGENAU, Premonstratensian Church of St Nicholas, page 62.
   The church appears to have been completed in 1425; the nave, eleven bays, dates from the first half of the 14th century; no transept, short choir with apse closed on five sides.

HEIDELBERG, Jesuit Church, page 69, plates 65, 66.

HÖCHST, Monastic Church of St Justinus, page 16.
   The Carolingian church had by way of choir a rectangular crossing transversally placed and a semicircular apse as sanctuary; also transept-like lateral units, accessible through low arches, with east apses. The monastic church of St Alban in Mainz had a similar type of choir. St Justinus' was rebuilt with alterations in 1090; the choir and the sanctuary underwent a Late Gothic restoration in 1443–64.

KNECHTSTEDEN, Premonstratensian Church, page 34, plates 170–173.

KOLMAR, Dominican Church, plates 30, 31.

KOLMAR, Abbey Church of St Martin, page 61, plates 32–34.

LAUTENBACH, Abbey Church, page 36.
The upper parts of the westwork were considerably restored in the 19th century. The church was no doubt to have had two towers; their lower stages flank a well-preserved porch three bays wide and two deep with two outer piers and two inner columns carrying a cross-arched vault which dates from the middle of the 12th century; the ribs have a right-angled profile with a sturdy round moulding.

LIMBURG AN DER LAHN, Collegiate Church of St George, page 51, plates 132–139.

LORSCH, Monastic Church, page 14, plate 100, fig. 4.
The westwork of the Carolingian church, extended upwards in 1025, was heavily damaged by fire in 1090. When the church was rebuilt a small atrium was added in front flanked at the entrance by two towers, after the example of Hirsau; consecrated in 1130. Later in the 12th century it was replaced by a three-aisled narthex. The monastery and the church were completely destroyed by Spanish troops in 1621.

MAINZ, Cathedral, page 29, 47, plates 90–99.

MANNHEIM, Jesuit Church, page 69, fig. 28.

MARIA LAACH, Benedictine Abbey, page 33, plates 140–143.

MARMONTIER, Benedictine Church, page 36.

MÖNCHEN-GLADBACH, Benedictine Church, page 50, 58, plates 166, 167.
Considerably damaged in the last war, the church has been rebuilt with the nave triforium preserving its original form.

MOLSHEIM, Jesuit Church, page 68, plate 35.

MURBACH, Abbey Church, page 36, fig. 14.

NEUSS, St Quirinus, page 50, plates 168, 169, fig. 20.

OBERWESEL, Collegiate Church of Our Lady, page 65, plates 106–108.

OPPENHEIM, St Catherine, page 66, plates 101–105, fig. 26.

OTTMARSHEIM, Convent Church, page 21, plates 26, 27.

REICHENAU, Monastery Church, page 18, 21, plates 1–6, fig. 6.

REICHENAU, St George's, page 18, 22, plates 7–11.

REICHENAU, St Peter and St Paul, page 22, plates 12–16.

SCHAFFHAUSEN, Monastic Church of All Saints, page 32, fig. 13.
    Founded in the 11th century when it was dedicated to the Saviour.

SCHETTSTADT, Benedictine Monastery of St Fides, page 42, plates 28, 29.

SCHWARZRHEINDORF, Convent Church, page 38, plates 152–157.
    Cruciform double church with a semicircular apse and a low tower over the crossing.
The two storeys communicate through a small opening in the vault of the lower one as in the
archiepiscopal chapel of the Cathedral at Mainz. The church was built in 1149–1151 by the later
archbishop of Cologne Arnold II von Wied on his land. At his death in 1156 (he is buried
in the lower church) the edifice was converted by his sister into a convent church, extended
westwards and a stage added to the tower (1173); the interior has valuable wall paintings.

SELIGENSTADT, Abbey Church, page 16.

SPEYER, Cathedral, page 25, plates 67–75, figs. 10, 11.

ST KATHARINENTHAL, Church of Dominican Nuns, page 71, plate 64.

STEIN AM RHEIN, Monastery Church, plate 17.

STEINBACH, Abbey Church, page 16.

The photographs of Helga Schmidt-Glassner have been supplemented from the following sources: Staatliche Messbildanstalt, Berlin: 182, 183, 187 — Dr. Franz Stoedtner, Düsseldorf: 185, 189–191 — Prof. Dr. Ernst Gall, Munich: 186, 188.

THE PLATES

Xanten • Wesel

Duisburg • Essen

Roermond •
Werden •
Mönchen-Gladbach
Düsseldorf
Neuss • Gerresheim
RUHR

Knechtsteden •
Altenberg •

Brauweiler •
Aix-la-Chapelle •
Cologne •

Bonn • Schwarzrheindorf •

Heisterbach •

Marienstadt •

Maria Laach •

Andernach •
Coblenz •
LAHN
Limburg •

MOSEL
Oberwesel •

Trèves •
Eberbach • Wiesbaden •
Bingen • Höchst • Frankfurt
Mainz • Hanau
MAIN
NAHE
Oppenheim • Seligenstadt •

Worms •
Lorsch • Steinbach •
Limburg a. d. Haardt •
Ludwigshafen • Mannheim • Michelstadt •
Heidelberg
Speyer • NECKAR

Welssenburg •
Neuweiler •
St. Johann • Surburg •
Zabern • Hagenau • Karlsruhe •
Marmontier •

Molsheim •
Strassburg
Odilienberg • Eschau Lautenbach •
Offenburg •
Schlettstadt •

Kolmar •
Breisach •
Murbach • Freiburg •
Ottmarsheim •
Thann •

Basle •
Feldbach • Schaffhausen • Diessenhofen •
RHINE St. Katharinenthal Reichenau •
Stein am Rhein
Constance LAKE CONSTANCE

1 Reichenau, monastery-church at Mittelzell. Tower of the west choir dating from the time of Abbot Berno, 1030–1048

2 Reichenau, monastery-church at Mittelzell, together with the monastery buildings, seen from the north-east

3 Reichenau, monastery-church at Mittelzell. General view from the north. The church, the oldest parts of which in the choir and sanctuary were consecrated in 816, underwent many alterations during the 10th, 11th and 12th centuries. The eastern extremity was rebuilt 1447–1477

4 Reichenau, monastery-church at Mittelzell.
View from the south aisle into the west choir with the transept dating from the time of Abbot Berno, 1030–1048

5   Reichenau, monastery-church at Mittelzell. Nave looking east.
The pillars and windows of the nave were partly altered circa 1688; the imposts and arches of the arcades, together with the
painted wooden ceiling, were restored in the 19th century. The late Gothic rear wall of the sanctuary was built in 1447–1477

6   Reichenau, monastery-church at Mittelzell. The sanctuary was restored in late Gothic style 1447–1477

7 Reichenau, St George's Church at Oberzell. General view from the north–east.
A 9th-century church rebuilt towards the end of the 10th century

8   Reichenau, St George's Church, Oberzell, seen from the west with the vestibule built in the late 11th century in front of the
9th-century west apse

9   Reichenau, St George's Church, Oberzell, from the south

10   Reichenau, St George's Church at Oberzell.
Crypt, rebuilt from the cell of Abbot Hatto (died 823) with the altar over his tomb

11   Reichenau, St George's Church at Oberzell.
Nave looking east. The pillars date from the 9th century, the triforium and choir from the end of the 10th century

12 Reichenau, collegiate church of St Peter and St Paul, Niederzell, from the east.
Towers built during the 11th and 12th centuries over the side apses of the older structure dating from
the 8th and 9th centuries which were enclosed by right-angle walls

13   Reichenau, collegiate church of St Peter and St Paul, Niederzell, from the north-west. Built during the 11th and 12th centuries

14   Reichenau, collegiate church of St Peter and St Paul, Niederzell.
View into the nave (pillared basilica), dating from the 11th and 12th centuries, and the choir which was rebuilt at this period
on the 8th and 9th-century foundation walls. Vaulting, windows and decoration date from the 18th century (rococo)

15   Reichenau, collegiate church of St Peter and St Paul, Niederzell.
East apse of the sanctuary with 12th-century murals and window restored in late Gothic style

16 Reichenau, collegiate church of St Peter and St Paul, Niederzell.
Eleventh to 12th-century capitals and arcades on the north-west side of the nave

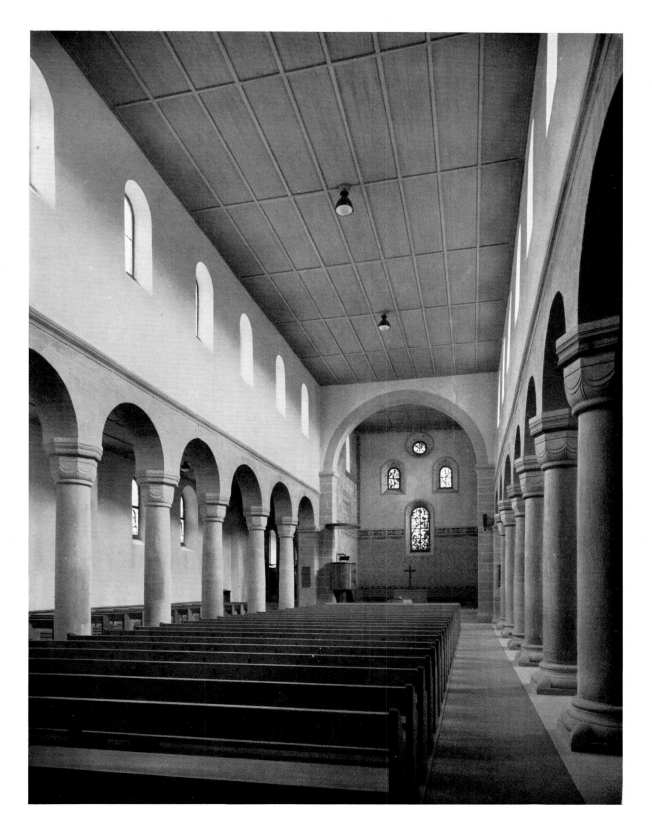

17　Stein am Rhein, monastery-church of St George.
Looking eastward into the nave and the choir with rectangular sanctuary, built circa 1100

18 Constance, cathedral. Vestibule crypt with three aisles below the sanctuary built by Bishop Lambert (995–1018). The four easternmost pillars (beside the altar) have recently been adjudged (H. Reiners) to be remains of the late 8th-century building

19   Constance, cathedral. Nave looking east. Pillared basilica dating from the third quarter of the 11th century, later rebuilt in the Gothic style; the pseudo-Gothic vaults were added between 1680 and 1683

20   Constance, cathedral. View of the west front. The Romanesque structure was rebuilt 1497–1511, the upper storeys were restored after a fire 1515–1524, and reconstructed in their present form with the central steeple 1844–1860

21   Constance, cathedral. Lower section of the west front built 1497–1511

22   Constance, cathedral.
Staircase, the so-called "Schnegg", in the northern arm of the transept ('St Thomas's Choir'), built by Master Antoni in 1438

23 Constance, cathedral.
Chapel of the Holy Sepulchre dating from the end of the 13th century, partially renewed 1560 and 1771 ff.

24 Basle, cathedral, west front. The two lower storeys of the northern (left) steeple date from the building consecrated in 1019, the lower part of the rest of the front from the 13th century, and the upper sections of the steeples
from the 15th century

25   Basle, cathedral. View of the north wall of the nave (1185 ff.) from the south-east, and into the second (outer) aisle added in the 14th century; the vaulting of the nave was added after 1356

26 Ottmarsheim, convent-church from the south-east.
The central structure dates from the first half of the 11th century, the side-buildings and the upper part of the extension of the west front (left) were added during the Gothic period. The higher roof of the central structure with the arched frieze dates from the 19th-century restoration

27 Ottmarsheim, convent-church. Central hall dating from the first half of the 11th century with view into the two-storey, square chancel

28   Schlettstadt, Benedictine monastery-church of St Fides from the south-west.
Built during the second half of the 12th century. The towers (four gables with diamond-shaped roofs) were added in 1890

29　Schlettstadt, Benedictine monastery-church of St Fides. Nave looking east.
Built during the second half of the 12th century, the triforium over the aisles was restored in 1890

30 Kolmar, Dominican church. View of the south-east aspect; begun 1283

31 Kolmar, Dominican church. View into the nave from the north-west; built circa 1300

32   Kolmar, collegiate church of St Martin. South-west tower from the north-west,
built at the beginning of the 14th century; the roof of the spire was rebuilt after a fire in 1572

33 Kolmar, collegiate church of St Martin. View into the nave looking east; begun after 1263; the choir was restored in the 14th century; late Gothic reticulated vaulting in the transept and intersection

34 Kolmar, collegiate church of St Martin. Choir and transept from the south.
Transept begun circa 1263, choir restored in the 14th century

35 Molsheim, Jesuit church. View into the nave looking east. Built in pseudo-Gothic style 1615–1618

36   Strassburg, cathedral. Distant view of the west front

37   Strassburg, close-up view of the west front; built 1277–1439

38 Strassburg, cathedral. South side-face of the nave, which was built circa 1250–1275; the ground-level extensions
between the buttresses were added during the 19th century

39 Strassburg, cathedral. View of the corner between the southern arm of the transept and the nave with the intersection tower restored during the 19th century. Between the nave and the southern transept (12th/13th centuries) is St Catherine's Chapel built 1331–1349. The remaining buildings were added during the 19th century

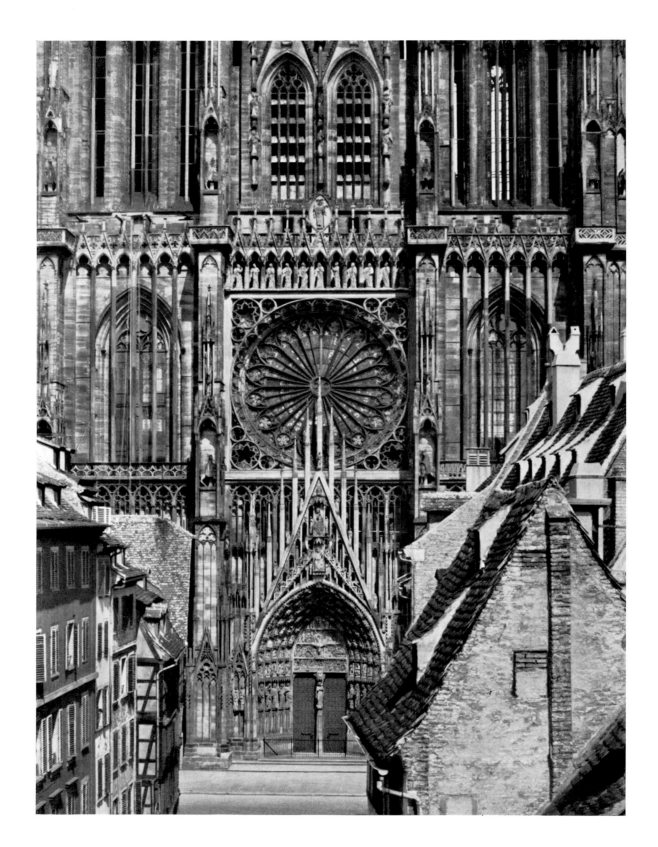

40 Strassburg, cathedral.
Lower part of the west front with centre door and rose window, begun in 1277 by Erwin of Steinbach

41   Strassburg, cathedral. South door of the west front, 1277 ff.

42   Strassburg, cathedral. Door of the south transept, first half of the 13th century

43 Strassburg, cathedral. Southern arm of the transept with the Pillar of Judgement (?); on the right in the east wall the entrance to St Andrew's Chapel; in the background the two tall pillars at the intersection of the nave and transepts; built between the end of the 12th and early 13th centuries

44 Nave with view into the late Romanesque choir dating from the end of the 12th century. The nave and aisles were
built circa 1250–1275, the vaulting restored 1459–1475

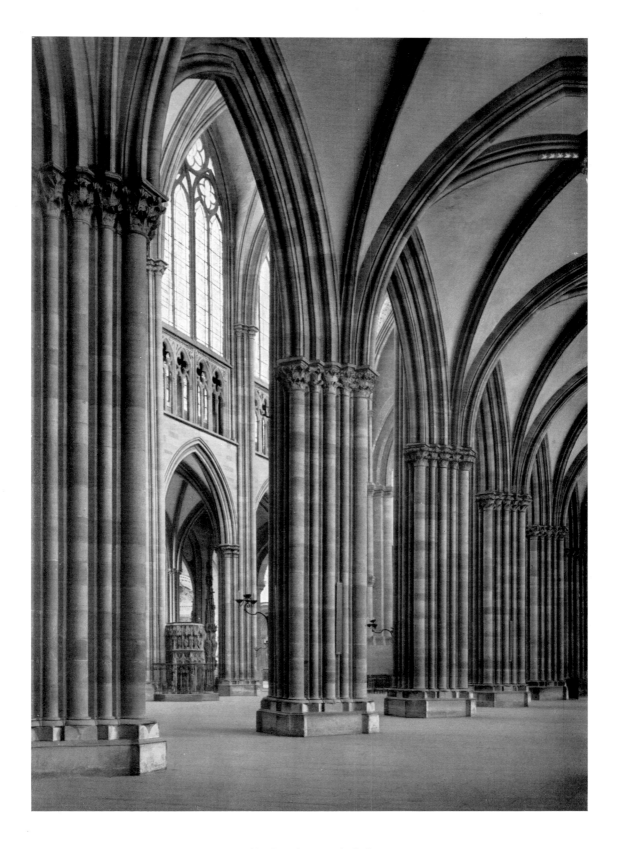

45   Strassburg, cathedral.
View from the south aisle looking north-east into the nave dating from 1250–1275

46   Strassburg, St Thomas's Church
(former monastery of Scottish monks) from the north-west. West wing 1230 ff., the second tower 1366

47 Strassburg, St Thomas's Church (former monastery of Scottish monks).
View into the nave looking south-east. Vestibule added circa 1330

48 Breisach, collegiate church of St Stephen. General view from the south-west.
Built between circa 1200 and the end of the 15th century. Severely damaged during the last war

49   Breisach, collegiate church of St Stephen. General view from the south-east

50 Breisach, collegiate church of St Stephen. View into the nave looking east.
Nave circa 1200, choir after 1300, rood-screen circa 1500. Restored after the last war

51 Breisach, collegiate church of St Stephen.
View into the early 14th-century sanctuary, with the high altar, dating from 1523–1526

52   Freiburg im Breisgau, cathedral from the south-east.
Built as a parish church from the beginning of the 13th century to 1513

53   Freiburg im Breisgau, cathedral from the west. The tower was built circa 1270–1350

54 Freiburg im Breisgau, cathedral. View of the sanctuary with gallery and ring of chapels, built 1354–1513. Balustrades and buttress-spires replaced in the 18th and 19th centuries

55   Freiburg im Breisgau, cathedral. South side of the nave and west tower from the south-east;
built during the second half of the 13th and beginning of the 14th centuries

56 Freiburg im Breisgau, cathedral. Entrance to the vestibule on the ground floor of the west tower, begun circa 1300

57   Freiburg im Breisgau, cathedral. Inner door of the vestibule on the ground floor of the west tower, circa 1300

58   Freiburg im Breisgau, cathedral. View into the nave looking east towards the choir. Building was begun before the
mid-13th century; the nave was finished at the beginning of the 14th century; the choir was built 1354–1513

59 Freiburg im Breisgau, cathedral. South-east section of the entrance to the choir, begun 1354

60   Freiburg im Breisgau, cathedral. View into the south arm of the transept, which was begun in late Romanesque form at
the beginning of the 13th century. In front of the south wall, part of the rood loft erected 1579–1589 and transferred to this
position as a choir gallery in 1789

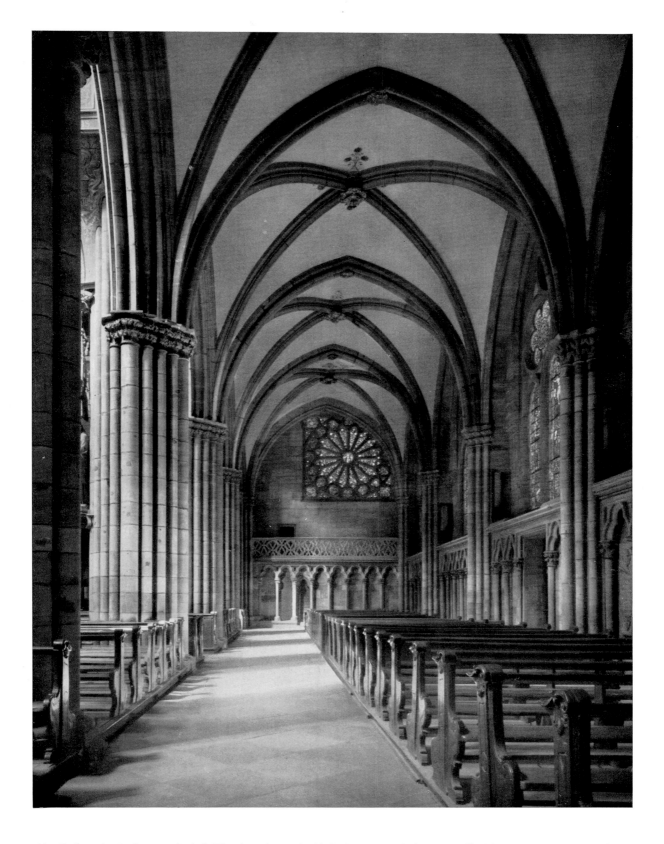

61 Freiburg im Breisgau, cathedral. View into the north aisle looking towards the west wall with a rose window dating from the third quarter of the 13th century

62   Freiburg im Breisgau, cathedral. Looking up into the roof of the spire of the west steeple richly decorated with tracery. The steeple was built towards the mid-14th century

63 Freiburg im Breisgau, cathedral. Late Gothic vaulting dating from 1510 over the choir and sanctuary, restored 1792

64 St Katharinenthal, church of Dominican nuns.
Built 1732-1735 by Johann Michael Beer. View into the sanctuary

65   Heidelberg, Jesuit church.
View into the central aisle of the "hall" nave from the west towards the choir, built 1712–1759

66   Heidelberg, Jesuit church, built since 1712, the façade (in the north) circa 1750,
the three upper storeys of the tower on the south side of the sanctuary 1868–1872

67   Speyer, cathedral from the north-east.
The eastern part of the building with the transept dates mainly from the time of Emperor Henry IV since circa 1080, the lower
sections of the side towers from the time of Conrad II an Henry III

68   Speyer, cathedral from the south. Built in the 11th and 12th centuries,
partially restored after damage (1689) in 1759 and 1772–1778; the western section (left) built by Heinrich Hübsch

69 Speyer, cathedral.
View of upper part of the east apse and sanctuary dating from the time of Emperor Henry IV.
Intersection tower rebuilt after fire in 1159 and 1759

70 Speyer, cathedral. Relief on pilaster in the east apse (ca. 1100).
Children are playing beneath palm-trees with lions and serpents (Messianic Kingdom of Peace according to Isaiah XI, 8)

71   Speyer, cathedral. Window in the south transept, ca. 1100

72 Speyer, cathedral. View of the north wall of the nave;
restoration carried out 1772–1778 within the system of rebuilding executed in the time of Henry IV and Henry V

73 Speyer, cathedral, nave and choir (the high altar originally stood not in the intersection but in the apse);
restoration carried out 1772–1778 within the system of rebuilding executed in the time of Henry IV and Henry V

74 Speyer, cathedral.
Crypt under choir and transept dating from the time of Conrad II with vaulting from the time of Henry IV

75 Speyer, cathedral.
View from the high altar in the intersection (fromerly in the apse) to the north side of the nave looking west

76 Worms, cathedral from the north-east.
Construction on the ground-plan of Bishop Burkhard's building (1000–1025) during the second half of the 12th century;
western section completed ca. 1225

77 Worms, cathedral.
East choir with the sanctuary (consecrated 1181) flanked by two towers, seen from the south

78 Worms, cathedral. East sanctuary, consecrated 1181

79 Worms, cathedral. Upper part of the front of the east sanctuary

80 Worms, cathedral. Decoration on the windows of the east sanctuary, consecrated 1181

81 Worms, cathedral. Dwarf-arched gallery on the front of the east sanctuary, consecrated 1181.
On the centre pillar a mason with an ape as a protective animal

82 Worms, cathedral.
Left: base of a projected pier with animal's head in the east choir (above) and of the second pillar of the north wall of the nave, ca. 1185 (below). Right; northeastern intersection pillar, St Juliana with angel and Satan

83 Worms, cathedral. Decoration at the foot of a projected pier in the east choir.

84 Worms, cathedral. View of the west section of the south-east choir tower, 1200–1225;
the side towers stand on foundations dating from Bishop Burkhard's building, 1000–1025

85 Worms, cathedral. West section, 1200–1225;
the side towers stand on foundations remaining from Bishop Burkhard's structure, 1000–1025

86 Worms, cathedral. View from nave into the east choir consecrated in 1181.
The high altar built 1741–1742 by Balthazar Neumann, the side altars ca. 1750 by Johann Peter Jäger

87 Worms, cathedral.
View from the west choir into the nave towards the east choir, end of the 12th century

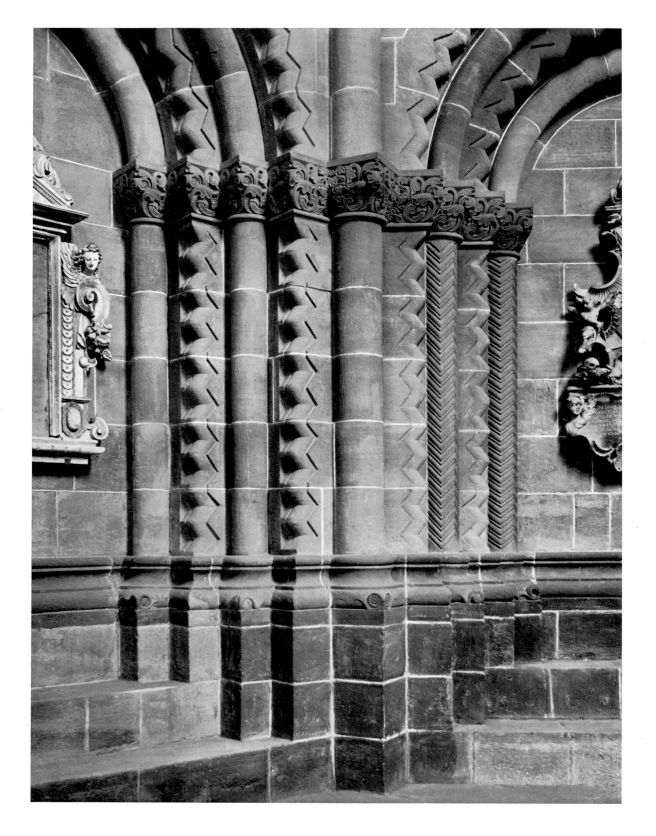

88 Worms, cathedral.
Decoration on the interior wall of the apse of the west sanctuary, ca. 1220

89   Worms, cathedral.
South door of the nave to the east of St Nicholas's Chapel, ca. 1289–1325

90   Mainz, cathedral from the north-west.
Built 1009–1239; upper parts of the west choir (right) rebuilt after fire by F. I. M. Neumann in 1767,
tower over the east intersection rebuilt by Cuypers 1869–1879. Restorations 1909–1916, 1925–1928 and after 1942

91 Mainz, cathedral from the east.
Built mainly between 1106 and 1137, the foundations of the side towers are remains of the building consecrated in 1036, the upper parts restored since 1870, the intersection tower 1869–1879

92 Mainz, cathedral.
South-east door on the east side next to the apse of the east sanctuary, completed 1137

93 Mainz, cathedral.
Capitals on the south-east door of the east sanctuary, completed 1137

94 Mainz, cathedral from the south-west.
Rebuilt in the early 13th century (consecrated 1239), the upper storey of the intersection tower restored in the Late Gothic,
remaining towers rebuilt by F. I. M. Neumann in 1767 after a fire

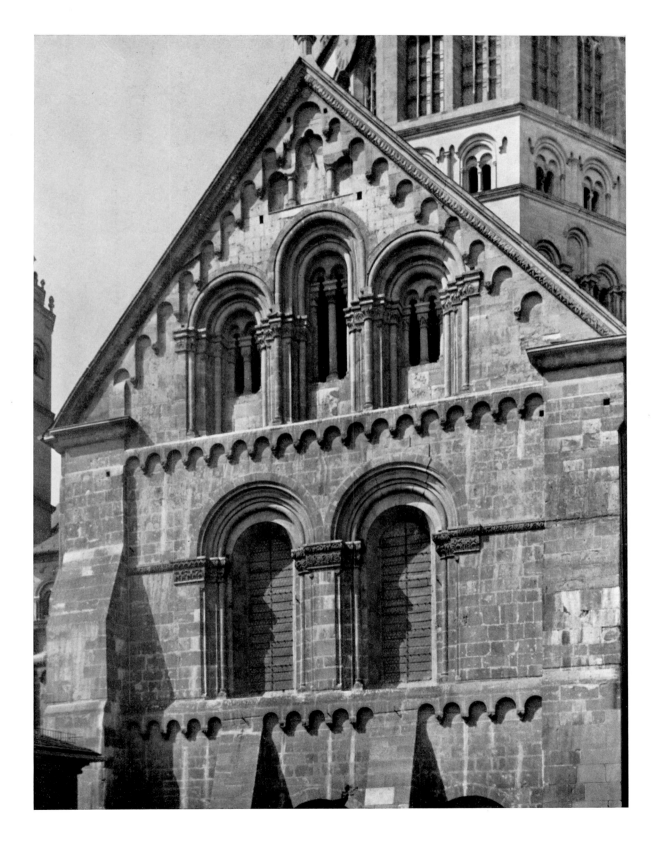

95 Mainz, cathedral.
South gable-front of the west transept dating from the early 13th century

96   Mainz, cathedral. View into the nave and the east choir;
built mainly between 1081 and 1137, the diagonal-ribbed vaulting dates from the beginning of the 13th century

97   Mainz, cathedral. View into the west choir from the nave.
The choir, which was built in the early 13th century, was consecrated in 1239 and 1243

98   Mainz, cathedral.
View of the capital area of the north-east intersection pillar in the west transept and the north outside wall of the nave;
some parts date from ca. 1200, restored 1925–1927

99 Mainz, cathedral.
View of the north wall of the nave, built between 1081 and 1137; vaulting from the beginning of the 13th century

100   Lorsch monastery, vestibule from the portico.
Built between 767 and 774; St Michael's chapel in the upper floor

101 Oppenheim, collegiate church of St Catherine from the north-west.
Romanesque west towers. The church was built ca. 1262–1370, the lofty west choir by Madern Gertener 1415–1439

102 Oppenheim, collegiate church of St Catherine.
View of the south face from the south-west; built in the 14th century before 1370; flying buttresses restored in 1890

103 Oppenheim, collegiate church of St Catherine.
View from the south-west of the south face with transept and intersection tower; built in the 14th
century before 1370

104   Oppenheim, collegiate church of St Catherine.
View through the south aisle looking east into the nave; built between 1262 and 1370.
Date inscription in the sanctuary of the south side chapel 1317

105   Oppenheim, collegiate church of St Catherine.
View through the nave looking east into the sanctuary; formerly parish church, built between 1262 and 1370

106 Oberwesel, collegiate church of Our Lady from the south-west.
Begun 1308, sanctuary consecrated 1331, nave completed round the mid-14th century. To the west of the church
St Michael's Chapel

107 Oberwesel, collegiate church of Our Lady from the east.
The sanctuary with the pentagonal rear wall was begun in 1308 and consecrated in 1331

108   Oberwesel, collegiate church of Our Lady.
View through the nave into the choir, before which stand the rood screen and the rood altar.
Built during the first half of the 14th century

109   Eberbach, Cistercian monastery-church from the south-east;
built 1170–1186; the chapels flanking the nave were added in the 14th century

110 Eberbach, Cistercian monastery-church.
View of the rectangular sanctuary from the north-east. Pilaster-strips on the lower part of the east wall; the upper blind
arch is a relic of the Gothic tracery window put in ca. 1320 and replaced by two round-arched windows in 1935

111   Eberbach, Cistercian monastery-church from the south-west.
Transept and nave built ca. 1170–1186, the chapels on the south aisle date from the 14th century,
the roofs with the small tower over the intersection from 1746

112 Eberbach, Cistercian monastery-church.
View through the nave looking east towards the rectangular sanctuary, built 1170–1186;
the upper window in the east wall dates from 1935 and replaces a Gothic tracery window

113 Eberbach, Cistercian monastery-church.
View from the transept towards the south-west

114 Trèves, cathedral from the north. Romanesque structure erected during the 11th and 12th centuries on Late Antique foundations dating from the 4th century; part of the upper stages of the towers were added during the Gothic and Late Gothic periods;
the spires of the east steeples date from the 19the century

115   Trèves, cathedral. View of the east sanctuary with two side towers dating from the second half of the 12th century, completed in 1196; the upper stages of the towers restored round the mid-14th century; the spires date from the 19th century. Baroque treasure-house in the east added 1709–1716

116   Trèves, cathedral and church of Our Lady from the west.
The west front of the cathedral, which was restored round the mid–11th century, was completed before 1121.
The church of Our Lady, one of the oldest Gothic buildings, was completed ca. 1253

117 Trèves, cathedral (left) and church of Our Lady (right) from the south-west

118 Trèves, cathedral, lower gallery on the southern section of the west front, completed before 1121

119 Trèves, cathedral. Southern upper part of the west front, completed before 1121

120   Trèves, cathedral. Crypt under the east choir, begun shortly after the mid-12th century;
the four eastern pillars were restored in the first half of the 13th century

121   Trèves, cathedral. View of the south side of the central aisle in front of the intersection.
The Romanesque nave was rebuilt in Gothic style in the early 13th century;
the transept and rear walls of the upper apertures were rebuilt after a fire in 1717

122   Trèves, cathedral.
View from the sanctuary of the Late Romanesque east choir into the nave towards the apse of the west choir consecrated in 1121.
Parts of the building dating from the 11th–12th centuries were restored in the 13th and 18th centuries

123   Trèves, cathedral. View from the central aisle eastwards into the choir that was finished in 1196.
The nave was rebuilt in the 13th and 18th centuries

124   Trèves, church of Our Lady from the south-east.
Building was begun after 1235 and finished in 1253. On the right the cathedral

125   Trèves, church of Our Lady.
View from the south transept looking south-east into the sanctuary; begun after 1235, finished in 1353

126   Trèves, collegiate church of St Paulinus. West door ca. mid-18th century

127   Trèves, collegiate church of St Paulinus from the west.
Built by Josef Walter and Johann Seitz 1734–1757 after a plan by Johann Balthazar Neumann

128   Trèves, collegiate church of St Paulinus
View into the entrance of the choir from the south-west

129 Trèves, collegiate church of St Paulinus.
View of the interior looking east towards the choir; built 1734–1757. Ceiling paintings by Christoph Thomas Scheffler

130   Coblenz, collegiate church of St Castor from the south-east.
Mainly rebuilt during the 12th and 13th centuries; the lower walls of the transept fronts and parts of the two lower stages of the
western section are relics of the old 9th-century building

131 Coblenz, collegiate church of St Castor from the west.
Parts of the two lower stages are relics of the 9th-century building, the towers were added in the 12th and 13th centuries

132 Limburg an der Lahn, collegiate church of St George from the north-west.
Begun ca. 1220, consecrated 1235

133   Limburg an der Lahn, collegiate church of St George. West front.
Begun ca. 1220, towers completed after 1235

134 Limburg an der Lahn, collegiate church of St George from the north-east.
Built ca. 1220 to 1235, the towers on the south transept were added 1863–1865

135 Limburg an der Lahn, collegiate church of St George.
Upper part of the sanctuary from the south-east; consecrated 1235

136 Limburg an der Lahn, collegiate church of St George.
View into the nave and choir from the south-west; begun ca. 1220, consecrated 1235

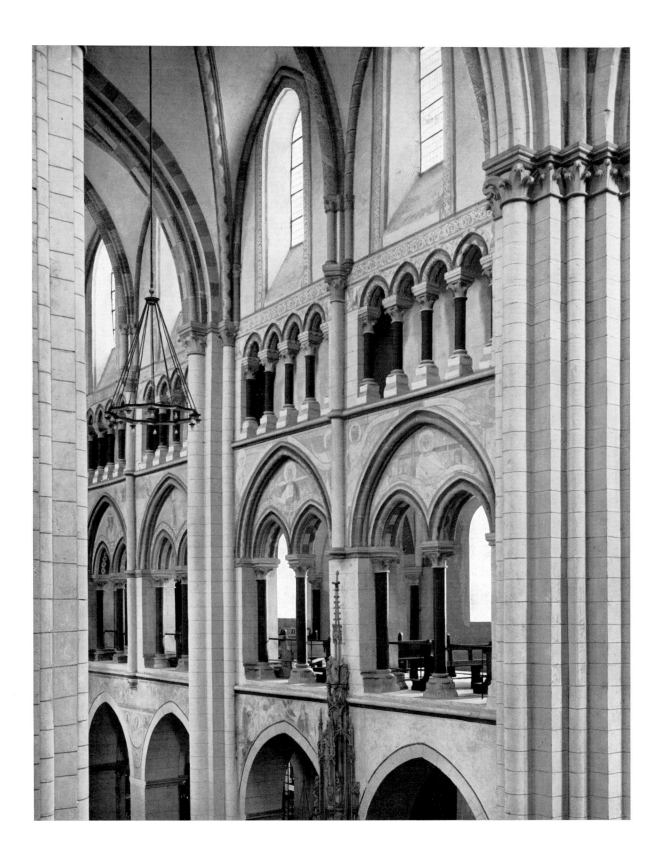

137 Limburg an der Lahn, collegiate church of St George.
View of the two double bays of the north side of the nave

138   Limburg an der Lahn, collegiate church of St George.
View of the west wall of the south transept from the east; consecrated 1235

139   Limburg an der Lahn, collegiate church of St George.
View into the north transept from the south-west; consecrated 1235

140   Maria Laach, Benedictine abbey from the north-west;
built between 1093 and the beginning of the 13th century

141 Maria Laach, Benedictine monastery-church.
West section with atrium from the north-west; mainly built between 1130 and the beginning of the 13th century

142   Maria Laach, Benedictine abbey.
Entry to the atrium in front of the west section; built at the beginning of the 13th century

143   Maria Laach, Benedictine Abbey.
Atrium in front of the west face, built at the beginning of the 13th century

144 Bonn, collegiate church from the south-east.
East parts finished 1166 as extension of an older building, transept end of the 12th century, window of the apse Late Gothic

145   Bonn, collegiate church from the north.
Nave dates from beginning of the 13th century, partially renewed after fire in 1239. Spire of the intersection steeple built
after 1590

146 Bonn, collegiate church.
Dwarf-arched gallery on the south transept with view of the south exterior of the nave (upper row of windows). Early
13th century, partially restored after fire in 1239

147   Bonn, collegiate church.
Crypt under the east choir seen from the south-west, ca. 1060–1070; the east section extended round the mid-12th century

148   Bonn, upper part of the two easternmost bays on the north side of the nave.
Beginning of the 13th century, partially restored after fire in 1239

149   Bonn, collegiate church.
View from the west into the nave and east choir. Nave built at the beginning of the 13th century, partially restored after fire in 1239. Choir partly 11th, partly 12th century, window of the apse Late Gothic

150   Bonn, collegiate church.
Brackets supporting the vaulting in the east choir; end of the 12th century

151   Bonn, collegiate church.
View from the south into the north transept, on the right the staircase to the choir; end of the 12th century

152 Schwarzrheindorf, convent-church (formerly manorial church) built 1149–1151.
Extended westward for the nuns after 1156; extra stage added to tower in 1173

153 Schwarzrheindorf, convent-church (formerly manorial church).
Ground floor looking east; the section behind the arcade was built 1149–1151, the part in front added as a western extension after 1156

154   Schwarzrheindorf, convent-church (formerly manorial church).
Upper stage of the east section seen from the north-west; built 1149–1151

155   Schwarzrheindorf, convent-church (formerly manorial church).
Ground floor of the east section seen from the west; built 1149–1151

156   Schwarzrheindorf, convent-church (formerly manorial church).
Dwarf-arched gallery on the south side seen from the south transept; built after 1156

157 Schwarzrheindorf, convent-church (formerly manorial church).
Outside dwarf-arched gallery on the north side on the staircase to the upper church; after 1156

158　Aix-la-Chapelle, former Palatine chapel (since 1801 cathedral church) from the south.
Only the centre part of the building dates from the Carolingian era, the superstructure was rebuilt in 1224, the baroque
roof in 1664. On the right the Gothic choir and a chapel added in the 14th and 15th centuries

159   Aix-la-Chapelle, former Palatine chapel.
Upper gallery, west half with the imperial seat from the north; consecrated in 805

160   Aix-la-Chapelle, former Palatine chapel. Middle of the central aisle, consecrated 805

161   Aix-la-Chapelle, former Palatine chapel. West gallery with the imperial seat, consecrated 805

162 Aix-la-Chapelle, former Palatine chapel. Apse of the new choir built 1355–1414 for the clergy of the chapter

163   Aix-la-Chapelle, former Palatine chapel.
South-east view of the choir built 1355–1414. Window tracery and figures on the flying buttresses restored

164   Brauweiler, Benedictine monastery-church.
West section, built before 1141; the chapel of St Michael on the upper storey consecrated 1141; spire added 1629

165   Brauweiler, Benedictine monastery-church.
View from the south-east of the north wall of the nave; built after 1141

166   Mönchen–Gladbach, monastery-church
Upper part of the north wall of the nave; built between 1200 and 1242

167 Mönchen-Gladbach, monastery-church.
View through the nave to the choir looking east. Nave built between 1200 and 1242, the choir later, consecrated 1275

168   Neuss, church of St Quirinus from the south-east.
Built during the first half of the 13th century, begun 1209

169 Neuss, church of St Quirinus.
View into the central aisle towards the choir in the east. Nave begun in 1209, the choir slightly later

170 Knechtsteden, Premonstrant church. South side of the nave with view of the transept; built 1138 ff.

171 Knechtsteden, Premonstrant church from the east. Built 1138 ff., the apse of the sanctuary restored after 1477

172 Knechtsteden, Premonstrant church. View into the north aisle and nave from the north-west; built 1138 ff.

173 Knechtsteden, Premonstrant church.
View from the east through the nave towards the west sanctuary; built 1138 ff.

174   Essen, ladie's collegiate church.
View from the east through the hall of the nave (1375 ff.) towards the west nuns' gallery;
built towards the end of the 10th century

175 Essen, ladie's collegiate church.
View of west section (end of the 10th century) with restored roof, of the atrium (left),
and the nave restored in Gothic style in 1375 ff.

176 Werden, monastery-church from the north-west.
Built 1256–1275; the west side still contains a few relics of the old structure erected in 943 as a parish church

177　Werden, monastery-church from the north-west.
View into the nave and east choir from the west; built 1256–1275

178   Altenberg, Cistercian church from the east.
Built 1255 ff., the choir consecrated 1287, the transept finished ca. 1300

179   Altenberg, Cistercian church from the west.
Nave completed shortly after consecration in 1379

180　Altenberg, Cistercian church.
View from the east into the north aisle and nave, built during the 14th century till after 1379

181 Altenberg, Cistercian church.
View from the west into the nave, the choir and the sanctuary; built from 1255 to shortly after 1379, starting from the east

182   Xanten, collegiate church. West front. Appearance before damage suffered in the last war.
Begun before 1190, lower storeys of the towers completed 1213, the three upper storeys of the towers built during the Gothic
period, the great central window put in at the beginning of the 16th century

183 Xanten, collegiate church. View from the south aisles into the western bay of the nave before the damage suffered during
the last war. The western part of the nave was not completed until 1559 (after a plan dating from ca. 1263); the west face is
Romanesque and dates from 1190–1213, but was partially restored during the Late Gotic period

184   Cologne, St Maria in Capitolio.
View of the sanctuary from the north-east, built in the mid-11th century, rebuilt ca. 1200; the Hirtz chapel added in
1493, the sacristy in ca. 1500; severely damaged during the last war

185   Cologne, St Maria in Capitolio.
View towards the north-east into the triapsal choir prior to damage suffered during the last war. The lower part of the structure dates from the mid–11th century, the upper part of the sanctuary and the vaulting from ca. 1200

186   Cologne, Great St Martin's from the north-west.
Built in the 10th century, rebuilt towards the end of the 12th and before the middle of the 13th; tower restored after fire
in 1378, west corner turret rebuilt during the 19th century. Severely damaged during the last war

187   Cologne, Great St Martin's from the north

188 Cologne, Apostles' Church.
View of the triapsal choir from the east; built after 1192; severely damaged during the last war

189   Cologne, St Pantaleon's.
View of the west side from the south-west; laid down towards the end of the 10th century; the west porch, the corner towers above the side cornices and the main tower were rebuilt in the 19th century

190 Cologne, St Gereon's from the south-west. The central structure was rebuilt on Late Roman foundations 1219–1227, the long choir on the east side (right), which was added in the 11th century, was extended to the east along with the towers round the middle of the 12th century. Partially destroyed during the last war

191 Cologne, St Gereon. South side of the nave.
Rebuilt 1219–1227 on Late Roman foundations dating from about the end of the 4th century

192 Cologne, cathedral. View of the west side from the north-west; begun ca. 1350, the north tower was only taken to the height of the aisle, the south tower to the third storey (1437), the rest was built 1842–1880 according to the original plan

193   Cologne, cathedral from the south-east.
Begun 1248, the choir was consecrated in 1322; the transept, nave and west towers were mainly built in 1842–1880 after old groundlines and elevations

194   Cologne, cathedral. South door of the west front; ca. 1375

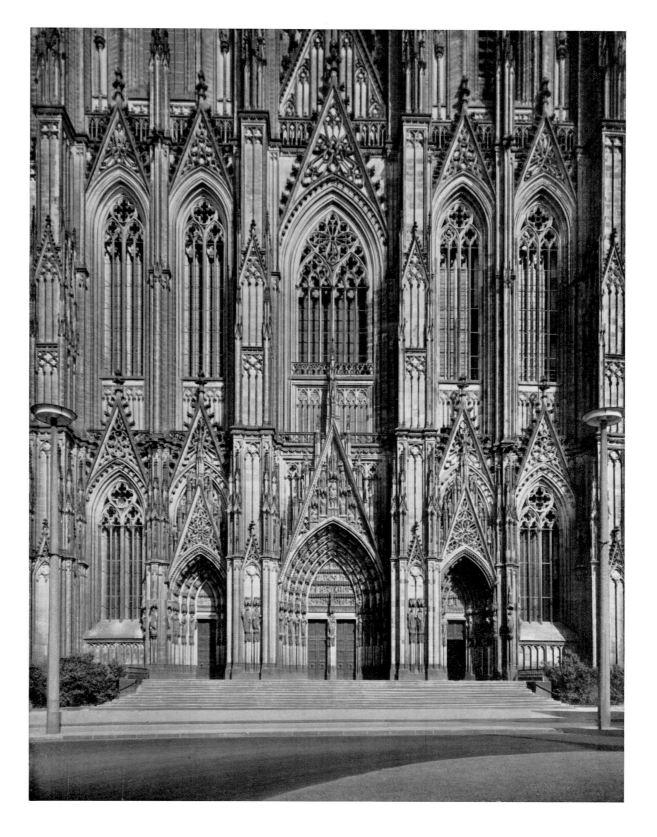

195 Cologne, cathedral. Lower part of the west front; only the south tower and the lower stage of the north tower
(1350 ff.) and the south door (ca. 1375) are old; the rest was built after the original plan 1842–1880

196   Cologne, cathedral. View from the west into the central aisle of the nave and the choir.
Only the choir (1248–1322) and the lower part of the nave (14th century) are old; from the triforium on the building dates
from 1842–1880. Partially destroyed during the last war

197 Cologne, cathedral. View from the west into the choir; built 1248–1322

198　Cologne, cathedral. View from the north-east into the south transept and the eastern half of the nave;
mainly new building from 1842–1880 down to the lower pillars

199 Cologne, cathedral. View from the north transept into the five-aisled nave; only the side aisles (14th century) are old; the central aisle was built 1842–1880. Partially destroyed during the last war

200   Cologne, cathedral.
Flying buttresses on the south transept against the choir; built 1842–1880 after the pattern of the choir buttresses

DATE DUE

Cat. No. 23-221

BRODART, INC.